SLOW KNITTING

SLOW KNITTING

a journey from
sheep to skein to stitch

Hannah Thiessen

photography by Katie Meek

ABRAMS / NEW YORK

Editor: Cristina Garces
Designer: Danielle Young
Production Manager: Kathleen Gaffney

Library of Congress Control Number: 2016961378

ISBN: 978-1-4197-2668-2

Printed and bound in the United States
10 9 8 7 6 5 4

Abrams books are available at special discounts when purchased
in quantity for premiums and promotions as well as fundraising
or educational use. Special editions can also be created to
specification. For details, contact specialsales@abramsbooks.com
or the address below.

 ABRAMS
The Art of Books

195 Broadway
New York, NY 10007
abramsbooks.com

table of contents

9   **INTRODUCTION**

12   Creating a Slow Wardrobe

16   SOURCE CAREFULLY

21   **Yarn Profile:** Green Mountain Spinnery

25   **Pattern:** Hepatica Cowl by Carol Feller

30   **Yarn Profile:** Julie Asselin

34   **Pattern:** Tsuga Cardigan by Bristol Ivy

40   **Yarn for Thought:** Free Range

42   PRODUCE THOUGHTFULLY

49   **Yarn Profile:** Brooklyn Tweed

53   **Pattern:** Grow by Norah Gaughan

60   **Yarn Profile:** Quince & Co.

64   **Pattern:** Sheep Sorrel by Pam Allen

68   **Yarn for Thought:** Handmade

70   THINK ENVIRONMENTALLY

74   **Yarn Profile:** Bare Naked Wools

78   **Pattern:** Wild Grains by Jennifer Wood

90   **Yarn Profile:** Sincere Sheep

94   **Pattern:** Russian Sage by Julia Farwell-Clay

102   **Yarn for Thought:** Organic

104   EXPERIMENT FEARLESSLY

111   **Yarn Profile:** O-Wool

115   **Pattern:** Myrtus by Kirsten Kapur

120   **Yarn Profile:** Jill Draper Makes Stuff

124   **Pattern:** Spruce by Meghan Fernandes

128   **Yarn for Thought:** Innovation

130   EXPLORE OPENLY

135   **Yarn Profile:** Woolfolk

139   **Pattern:** Luma by Véronik Avery

148   **Yarn Profile:** mYak

152   **Pattern:** Rhodiola by Michele Wang

158   **Yarn for Thought:** Wanderlust

160   **BEYOND SLOW KNITTING**

165   **ABBREVIATIONS**

167   **SPECIAL TECHNIQUES**

168   **YARN RESOURCES**

171   **INDEX OF DESIGNERS**

174   **ACKNOWLEDGMENTS**

176   **ABOUT THE AUTHOR**

introduction

THE WORLD FEELS LIKE IT'S in constant movement these days. Timelines, deadlines, due dates—time rushes forward in a blur of tasks fulfilled and checked off and crossed out. Our desks are constantly littered with pages of magazines and books, piles of bills, invoices, notes, and lists. For those of us who knit, our fiber purchases add up, too, and quickly turn into swatches, samples, patterns, and projects, speeding into the hands of lucky loved ones. Long gone are the days of early knitting discoveries; the once slow, halting gesture of making a knit stitch now multiplies by the thousands, casting on, binding off—we become fly fishermen of the hat, sock, and sweater. We love the feeling of accomplishment as we come to the end of a project, and we carry the glow with us into the casting on of the next and the next, in quick succession.

Amid this constant buzz of distractions, obligations, and pressure to produce prolifically, I've found myself more and more entranced by the siren song of what I like to call "slow knitting." The concept of slow knitting encourages us to stop in our tracks, take a breather from our busy lives, and reevaluate what we consume, what we make. Like the slow food movement, which revolves around the idea that ingredients that are carefully and thoughtfully produced will result in better food, I believe that discovering the story behind my yarn and the materials I use in my making will result in better projects for the spirit, for the environment, and for the fiber community as a whole. When I embarked on this slow knitting journey, I found myself living by a few basic tenets:

SOURCE CAREFULLY

At its core, slow knitting is a celebration of craftsmanship—the time spent making an object is just as important as the object itself. Working from the ground up, that is, letting your materials dictate your pattern and not vice versa, allows you to be more thoughtful about your projects and how you use your time. It's about asking for the story behind the fiber you're buying and making choices based on what you're told.

Taking a moment to discover the history of your materials brings fresh life to processes that many knitters find burdensome, like swatching. Swatching is a process typically seen as an unavoidable nuisance standing in the way of getting to the real knitting. I used to be the type of knitter who dreaded working up a swatch. Now, I revel in the happiness that is winding and casting on the sample. Choosing quality fibers and taking the time to swatch carefully allows me to know at the review of a pattern which fibers are going to be the best fit—I no longer worry about choosing the right yarn for a project, because I am closely acquainted with every fiber on my shelf. Through the knitting of the swatch, we become old friends. A washed and blocked swatch reveals all, and by handling this piece of fabric, you learn its secrets.

MAKE THOUGHTFULLY

A slowly knit project takes as long as required. In order to cherish the time and effort involved in good craftsmanship, allow yourself to give up the idea of a "quick knit." Set no boundary for finishing—I no longer make promises to friends, coworkers, or family members regarding my knitting. If I choose to make a gift and give it for a birthday, new baby, or holiday, it is a decision I make for myself. If it is not completed in time, it will be eventually. Do not delude yourself that a knitted gift is less expensive. The currency here is time, and I urge those who make things to evaluate carefully how they spend it.

THINK ENVIRONMENTALLY

Knitting is a process that relates to the natural world: Most fibers come from organic means, and those fleeces follow a yearlong journey from the farm to the finished skein in your hands. Taking cues from the life cycle of a fleece, knitting feels more comprehensive and cohesive when practiced in time with the changing seasons. I have found that by allowing my process to develop at its own pace and relate to the world around me, I experience the creation of my garments and projects more completely. The anticipation of cooler months gives me renewed excitement each fall, while the length of winter evenings aids the slow, steady progression of larger projects. Spring brings with it the excitement of warmer weather and the turn outdoors. This is the perfect time of year to begin spinning, with light breezes and sunshine to dry and fluff finished skeins that can later be dyed with the plants that bud and grow throughout the warmer seasons.

EXPERIMENT FEARLESSLY

Putting slow knitting into practice will allow you to muse over the simplicity of the stitches you know and rise to the challenge of using new techniques and materials. Take away the burden of perfection, and instead allow yourself to embrace or correct your mistakes as they come. Do not be lured by laziness or get swept up in haste, and do not be afraid to set aside something difficult and fix it later. A craftsperson's work is never perfect. It is made by human hands and therefore will have natural, beautiful flaws. Take pleasure in the slip of the yarn between your fingers, the pull of wool against wool. The twist of a cable or the surprising slant of a lace stitch is a tiny amusement against the background of the project.

EXPLORE OPENLY

Another important aspect of slow knitting is community building. Regardless of where, how, or when we start, knitters share common experiences. It is possible to travel halfway around the world and still carry on conversations with other knitters. The simultaneous experimentation and familiarity of the craft is like a secret language all its own—you only need to pick up needle and wool to speak it. Since knitters continue to develop skills and are eager to share them with others, it's easy to find friendly assistance when you need it, in person or through the vast online community.

Embracing the art of slow knitting is a promise to yourself to be more completely absorbed with the passion and love you have for this versatile and varied craft, and a commitment to engaging with creating a slow wardrobe. Move beyond the act of knitting as a task within a task. Although I often knit while watching television or listening to a book, in the most simple, quiet moments when nothing else is on in the background, I find myself thinking about the knitting itself as I go along, something that I have not done since those first few years of learning.

With this book, I challenge you to rediscover or enhance your own love of sticks and string by exploring your knitting in a new way. Source carefully, make thoughtfully, think environmentally, experiment fearlessly, and explore openly—the world of fiber awaits.

creating a slow wardrobe

One of the things that is most endearing about knitting as a hobby or passion is the ability to make garments that will last. I am so much more likely to darn a sock or sweater sleeve if I know that I worked to make the garment from scratch. More often than not, that piece is worn because it's also experienced heavy rotation in my wardrobe.

Knitting your own garments is a rewarding process that allows full customization of what fits you. While purchasing clothing sometimes presents an illusion of easiness, I have come to discover that it is more exhausting than it seems, and I value my time. Spending hours searching for the garment I have in mind, only to discover it in the wrong color, slightly off fit, or with a price tag beyond my means, is discouraging. I choose instead to use the hours potentially spent shopping in the comfort of my own home, creating custom, well-fitted pieces I know I will love to wear for years to come.

There are so many modern movements that pursue the idea that as individuals, we have the power to determine how the fashion industry operates, labels, and makes its clothes. Each May, Instagram is awash with #memademay hashtags, highlighting handmade wardrobe items made by crafters worldwide. In October, Karen Templer's "Slow Fashion October" project encourages makers and buyers to reconsider the sources of their garments and share what they have been working on. "Wovember" fills the month of November with awareness about wool. Slow knitting, of course, is a year-round meditation on the progress of our projects. Only by actively working against the principles of fast fashion in such ways do I feel we can make a difference and leave a legacy of textile possibilities open to future generations.

reflections on a slow wardrobe

Karen Templer, proprietor of Fringe Supply Co.

I've been a clotheshorse and fashion junkie my entire life, and I have always understood fashion as an art form and style as an act of creative expression. I was the typical kid who never properly appreciated all the beautiful clothes my mom made me, and the atypical kid who lived for the Saturday morning runway news on CNN. (Google Elsa Klensch, seriously.) I've also always understood that clothes could become special to you, souvenirs of a place or time in your life—the outfit you picked to boost your confidence upon your arrival at sleepaway camp for the first time, or the dress you were wearing the night your husband proposed. But I had no idea how many levels of meaning a garment could hold until I began to make my own in earnest.

As every knitter knows, we stitch our lives into our projects. A sweater can take weeks or months to complete, and when you put it on, you'll always be aware of the trips, waiting rooms, or cross-country moves the sweater accompanied you through. Learning to knit a few years ago led me back to sewing (after years of gradually forgetting most of what my mother had taught me), but before I really dusted off my machine, I enlisted my talented friend Alyssa to make me two garments that were beyond my skills—a dress for my brother's wedding and a tunic with a faced yoke and hand-stitched finish. Both of them were beautiful, and both were imbued with memories of working with Alyssa on them. Not fancy clothes, but genuinely one-of-a-kind. At the same time, I was filling my closet with sweaters made with my own two hands and their respective sets of memories, and slowly falling out of love with store-bought.

The more you think about these things, the more you tune in to the process. And it turns out, there's a whole other level beyond the making itself, which is where the yarn and fabric come from and how they came into your possession. I have a vest, for example, knitted of Hole & Sons wool, from British sheep I followed on Instagram for years before the farmer decided to make yarn from their fleece! I own multiple yarns produced by friends who worked directly with the farmers and mills to make something meaningful and unique for their shops, despite making no profit on it, and those stories and friendships will be part of whatever the yarns become. I cherish a top sewn from fabric a friend back in California sent me after I'd moved away to Tennessee, that she dyed in the natural indigo vat she worked so long and hard to bring to life. It's some of the best sewing I've ever done, so it represents both of our triumphs. The list goes on and on.

I remember the moment I realized that my lifelong relationship with clothes had changed irrevocably. My husband and I were in a J.Crew store (long one of my most reliable sources) and I was standing in the sale area, sliding hanger after hanger along the racks, unmoved. Even the lilac cardigan I'd coveted in photos—now more than half off!—stirred not an ounce of want, and not just out of concerns about what sort of far-away factory it might have been made in and whether the workers were paid a living wage (although of course there's always that). I just remember feeling so intensely, *these are just clothes*. I have the power to make *treasures*.

CHAPTER 1

source carefully

I HAVE BEEN KNITTING FOR a long time, a lot longer than the average knitter of my skill level. I learned when I was very small and kept it up by way of quick and simple projects throughout the years. Then, in my early twenties, I decided to dive in headfirst, spurred by a combination of loneliness and the terrible beauty of my first Midwestern winter. How humbled I was to discover in the first few years of actively working in the knitting industry that this was not the case for every one of the very best and brightest designers and fiber producers! Many crafters whose skills far exceeded my own had been knitting for a fraction of the time, yet they were much more comfortable whispering yarns into beautiful projects or patterns. The one thing they all had in common was that by indulging their passion through not only making, but also learning about the materials they used, they had gathered more knowledge in a much shorter period.

This quest to knitting knowledge is easily begun by forming a relationship with the fibers that you use. Wool, easily accessible in any local yarn store, is a wonderful place to start. First look at the yarn as a whole object made of a fiber. That fiber comes from somewhere—a sheep, in this case, but what kind of sheep? Each breed has its own merits. Where it comes from matters, too. Who feeds it? Who found this fiber and turned it into this yarn, and why did they choose this weight, this ply? Why did they blend it with another fiber, and what color was it before it was dyed? You can read the label or ask the yarn store owner for this information (I find yarn store owners are a bit like librarians who know where all the best books are hidden away). How do these qualities show in the skein in your hand? Weigh it, squish it, and smell it. Breathe in the lanolin, the barn, the spinning mill, the vinegar or clean, fresh scent of wool wash. Roll a single strand between your thumb and forefinger and admire the character. Let the wool convince you that it deserves to be yours, that it has earned a place in your home and in your future project.

All too often, I find the answers to these questions wanting, or missing, and leave a skein on a shelf. Yarn is not a lost puppy, looking for a home. Above all, it is a purchase, one that I see as a commitment not only of money, but also time. Knowing where it comes from matters, because you will be spending countless hours together—make sure you have found yourself in good company. The wide availability of information online has made obtaining this knowledge easier, along with the expert opinions of knitters from all over the world who have likely already spent time with this fiber. Knitting has the interesting cultural identity of being both a communal and solitary craft, and we can take both natures into account here by remembering that every yarn is not for every person.

When I encounter someone whose professional or personal identity sits firmly within the fiber world, particularly the working-with-wool camp, I love to ask them how they came about developing this identity. There is something supremely nostalgic about reliving your first few stitches, your initial projects, and the frustrations of learning, which remind us of everything that we love about knitting now. I love to see someone who has come so far in their knitting journey relive the beginning of it again, go back to a time when they had no idea how important this skill would become.

My own knitting story is fairly stereotypical, in a way. I learned from Mary Hal, an older shepherdess and fiber artist living in my community in rural central Kentucky. Occasionally, she would invite some of the "city kids" from her church over on Sunday afternoons to learn different crafty things: a bit of baking, a bit of spinning, and a lot of knitting. We learned on leftover wools from Mary Hal's extensive collection. At our first session, she handed each of us a pair of double-pointed needles she'd made from old dowels and a pencil sharpener, carefully sanded and oiled with lavender. They had a "10" written on them and fit perfectly in my hands. The smell of lavender always brings back my memory of these needles.

We moved away from Kentucky only a year or two after the lessons began, and my knitting became less and less, though I never fully let it go. Then, in college, a boyfriend bought me a subscription to a knitting magazine as a present. That subscription, combined with the recent rise of the Internet knitting culture and friends who were eager to learn from my skills, opened the door to me rediscovering my love of knitting. Eventually, I dropped out of school to pursue my love of wool and sheep.

Mary Hal's early teachings about the sustainability, the benefits, and the history of wool still stick with me. She taught me that the best wool comes from sheep raised by those with yarn in mind (although there is plenty to be said for dual-use flocks). Stress shows in a fleece's color and strength, in the shine and crimp. Healthy, happy sheep produce beautiful fibers, which in turn become beautiful yarns, and beautiful projects. Each finished skein maintains this filament line of the heritage, breeding, and history of the wool. Knitting, for me, is about remembering my own story, but also the story of the sheep and the people who raise them. Casting on with a good wool pulls my memories of spending time in the barn, the smell and feel of spinning in the grease, the soft slick of lanolin, and the scent of lavender oil. There is simply no better fiber to reach for when I want to remember where I discovered myself.

next steps

Careful sourcing can seem like a big undertaking, so I recommend starting small by combing through your stash before purchasing new materials. As fiber appreciators, it's easy for us to be overzealous about our passion and then feel overwhelmed by stashes that exceed what we believe we could ever truly conquer. Analyzing what we have already collected is a wonderful first step toward practicing careful yarn sourcing.

First, look beyond the yarn to the fiber. Yarn is born in a barn and travels for years on hoof before it ever becomes a single stitch. Where and how the animals are raised, what genetic makeup they have, and the individuals caring for them are key ingredients in some of my favorite wools. Look at what you already have in your stash and take note of any holes you'd like to fill. Then, read up on different breeds and test out any new fibers on smaller projects before making larger stash commitments. Because this process can quickly result in a large stash of solo skeins, I have adapted a revolving door strategy: If a yarn doesn't beg me to cast on within the year, it goes to a new home (sell, gift, or donate—just let it go!).

Our knitting time is not limitless, and keeping a yarn we don't love only means that it will be neglected and passed over continually for better prospects. It also means that we have less space for experimenting with new fibers. Sort through, cull generously, and release yourself from guilt by knowing you'll be using what you've kept. There are many yarns in the world, so don't hesitate to let one go in favor of another.

green mountain spinnery

When I first began speaking about this book with those who would later grace these pages with their designs, it was suggested to me almost immediately that I contact Green Mountain Spinnery, a mill in rural Vermont that built its business on producing carefully sourced, thoughtfully produced, and environmentally minded yarns. Green Mountain Spinnery has become synonymous with making things the right way, the slow way—they are rooted in the consciousness of the industry as an entity dedicated to celebrating wool in the process of making and selling yarn.

It is rare, these days, to find a business that started with such a sense of community from the very beginning. In the late seventies, weaver Claire Wilson attended a study group on sustainability. The group's focus shifted to the rich textile history of upper New England (namely Maine) and the loss of textile production facilities in the area. Claire and two other attendees, Diana Wahle and David Ritchie, joined forces with the intention of starting a small-production mill that could provide a local alternative to the influx of imported textiles flooding the market. They wanted to go back to basics. Elizabeth "Libby" Mills, a weaver, knitter, and local shepherd with a passion for sustainability (and friend of Claire), joined in quickly thereafter. They applied for a business loan from an organization supporting state and local businesses and earned funding from a group of private community members to help with the business's start, the purchase of mill equipment, and building.

They purchased a recently closed gas station and worked to source mill machinery. While finding vintage operational machinery was possible, learning to operate the machines, some of which had been built fifty or sixty years prior, required expertise they did not have. They spent time with experts still working at other mills in operation in North America and the United Kingdom, purchasing machines secondhand and planning their business piece by piece. With the eventual hire and help of Ray Phillips, a veteran mill operator, they were able to begin the work of operating a running mill.

Thirty-five years later, Green Mountain Spinnery continues to weather the changing winds of the commodity-based wool market. The first yarn produced—a naturally colored wool from local shepherds in five tones—is long out of production, but the Spinnery continues to offer a range of beautiful yarn selections featuring alpaca, mohair, wool, and organic cotton sourced in the United States. In addition to producing a line of yarns with their own label, the mill also produces custom-spun yarns for private label brands.

Each yarn produced fully embodies the history and mission of Green Mountain Spinnery: to be an easily accessible resource for those who want to make beautiful, sustainable yarns. Some wool comes from small-scale production farms, taking a year's single yield and turning it into wool that will be sold skein by skein, from farmer's hands directly to local buyer's needles. Other yarns they produce grace the shelves of yarn stores around the world, refined and simultaneously rustic, spun to the exacting preferences of discerning wool experts. Green Mountain Spinnery's story is the story of wool from start to finish in the purest form: It starts with a fleece and ends with a yarn.

Their own yarn selection has expanded as well with time, and now includes over fourteen individual yarns, plus a rotating menu of limited edition wools produced by smaller farms. Incorporating fleeces sourced from farms across New England from Rambouillet, Columbia, Targhee, Friesian, Corriedale, Montadale, and Romney sheep, Weekend Wool is a wonderful example of a blended yarn that showcases the individual attributes of these breeds—color, crimp, texture, and sheen, all blended with the soft heathery tones of different fleeces. Dyed in Philadelphia in a range of deep, beautiful shades, or even left neutral, this yarn is a lofty worsted weight that knits up admirably into pert cables or snuggly

brioche. Perhaps what makes this yarn most attractive is the way that it combines the diverse wool heritage of its place of conception: New England's colorful history is referenced in every lively skein.

It is no wonder to me that in a time where many knitters are turning their needles toward yarns that are sustainable, locally sourced, and beautifully made, Green Mountain Spinnery continues to be synonymous with the spirit in which it started. The dream of creating a mill where the history of the region could be highlighted through locally produced and sourced yarns has grown into an enterprise that celebrates North American wool in new and innovative ways. Each yarn is carefully crafted with attention to detail and the acknowledgment that it has been passed down: from the weathered, working hands of farmers past to the clicking needles of knitters present.

Hepatica Cowl

Designed by Carol Feller

This cowl pattern perfectly embraces the slightly rustic feel of Green Mountain Spinnery's Weekend Wool. This yarn is a true embodiment of the co-op from which it comes: It pulls together different sheep breeds sourced from all over New England. Dyed in an array of rich heathered tones or left natural, this yarn bares its soul in every stitch.

By combining simple textured stitches with wedges of short rows, Hepatica showcases the loft and slight halo on this hefty two-ply yarn. Knit flat side to side, this cowl is easily worn doubled up to keep away the chill or in a casual single loop. While you can use any short-row method you prefer, designer Carol Feller recommends that you try the German short-row method (see page 27), which yields discrete directional shifts.

FINISHED MEASUREMENTS
54" (137 cm) circumference x 10" (25.5 cm) tall

YARN
Green Mountain Spinnery Weekend Wool [100% wool; 140 yards (128 meters) / 2.12 ounces (60 grams)]: 4 hanks #7765 Deep Lake

NEEDLES
One pair straight needles size US 8 (5 mm)

Change needle size if necessary to obtain correct gauge.

NOTIONS
Crochet hook size US H-8 (5 mm); waste yarn; tapestry needle

GAUGE
16 sts and 29 rows = 4" (10 cm) in Texture Pattern

ABBREVIATION
DS: Double Stitch (see German Short Rows on page 27)

STITCH PATTERNS
TEXTURE PATTERN (see Chart)
(multiple of 3 sts + 8)
Row 1 (RS): Slip 1, knit to end.
Row 2: Slip 1, k2, purl to last 3 sts, k3.
Row 3: Slip 1, k2, p2, *k1, p2; repeat from * to last 5 sts, p2, k3.
Rows 4 and 5: Slip 1, k4, *p1, k2; repeat from * to last 3 sts, k3.
Row 6: Repeat Row 3
Rows 7–10: Repeat Rows 3–6.
Rows 11 and 12: Repeat Rows 3 and 4.

RIGHT WEDGE (see Chart)
Row 1 (RS): Slip 1, k34, turn.
Row 2: DS, purl to last 3 sts, k3.
Row 3: Slip 1, k2, [p2, k1] 9 times, turn.
Row 4: DS, [k2, p1] 8 times, k5.
Row 5: Slip 1, k4, [p1, k2] 6 times, p1, k1, turn.
Row 6: DS, [k1, p2] 7 times, k3.
Row 7: Slip 1, k2, [p2, k1] 5 times, p2, turn.
Row 8: DS, k1, [p1, k2] 5 times, k3.
Row 9: Slip 1, k4, [p1, k2] 3 times, p1, turn.

Row 10: DS, [p2, k1] 4 times, k2.
Row 11: Slip 1, k2, [p2, k1] twice, p1, turn.
Row 12: DS, p1, k2, p1, k5.
Row 13: Slip 1, k4, turn.
Row 14: DS, p1, k3.

LEFT WEDGE (see Chart)
Row 1 (RS): Slip 1, knit to end.
Row 2: Slip 1, k2, p32, turn.
Row 3: DS, p1, [k1, p2] 10 times, k3.
Row 4: Slip 1, k4, [p1, k2] 8 times, p1, turn.
Row 5: DS, [k2, p1] 8 times, k5.
Row 6: Slip 1, k2, [p2, k1] 7 times, p1, turn.
Row 7: DS, [k1, p2] 7 times, k3.
Row 8: Slip 1, k4, [p1, k2] 5 times, turn.
Row 9: DS, k1, [p1, k2] 5 times, k3.
Row 10: Slip 1, k2, [p2, k1] 4 times, turn.
Row 11: DS, [p2, k1] 4 times, k2.
Row 12: Slip 1, k4, p1, k2, p1, k1, turn.
Row 13: DS, p1, k2, p1, k5.
Row 14: Slip 1, k2, p2.
Row 15: DS, k4.

TEXTURE PATTERN

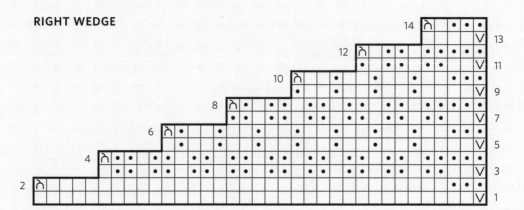

Knit on RS, purl on WS.

Purl on RS, knit on WS.

Slip 1 knitwise wyib.

DS (Double Stitch)

3-st repeat

RIGHT WEDGE

LEFT WEDGE

SPECIAL TECHNIQUES
CROCHET PROVISIONAL CAST-ON

This cast-on method uses waste yarn and a crochet hook to create a crochet chain that wraps a stitch around your knitting needle at the same time. It is not necessary to know how to crochet to use this method.

Make a slipknot with waste yarn and place it on the crochet hook.

Hold the needle in your left hand, pointing up, and the crochet hook in your right hand; hold both ends of the yarn behind the needle with your left hand, with the working end of the yarn over your index finger. *Take the crochet hook across the front of the needle, go under the working end of the waste yarn from left to right, catch the yarn, and draw it through the loop on the crochet hook to create 1 stitch on the needle; take the working end of the yarn over the tip of the needle to the back again. Repeat from * until you have cast on the required number of stitches on your needle. Cut the yarn and draw the tail through the loop on the crochet hook to fasten off. Tie a small knot in the tail to indicate which end of the cast-on to undo to unravel it. Change to working yarn for first row.

When ready to work the live sts, unravel the chain by loosening the end with the knot and "unzipping" the chain, placing the live sts on a spare needle.

GERMAN SHORT ROWS

Work to specified turning point, then turn work. Slip 1 stitch purlwise to right-hand needle with yarn in front. Pull yarn over top of needle to back, creating a double stitch (DS) on the right-hand needle. If the next stitch to be worked is a knit stitch, leave yarn at back, and keep yarn tight when working the first stitch to ensure the double stitch stays in place. If the next stitch to be worked is a purl stitch, bring yarn to the front, ready to work the next stitch.

When short rows are completed, knit or purl the two legs (the one created by taking the yarn over the needle and the original slipped stitch) of the double stitch together. When counting stitches, always count the double stitch as a single stitch.

KITCHENER STITCH

Note: The first and last 3 sts at each edge of the Cowl are worked in Garter stitch, which requires a slightly different way of working Kitchener stitch. Full details for grafting the Cowl are given here.

Using a blunt tapestry needle, thread a length of yarn approximately 4 times the width of one piece. Hold the pieces to be joined wrong sides together, with the needles holding the sts parallel, both ends pointing to the right. Work from right to left.

Set-Up

With right sides facing and live stitches from cast-on edge at the bottom (front needle), insert tapestry needle into first stitch on front needle as if to purl, pull yarn through, leaving stitch on needle.
Insert tapestry needle into first stitch on back needle as if to purl, pull yarn through, leaving stitch on needle.

Step 1

Insert tapestry needle into first stitch on front needle as if to knit, pull yarn through and remove stitch from needle.
Insert tapestry needle into first stitch on back needle as if to purl, pull yarn though, leaving stitch on needle.

Step 2

Insert tapestry needle into first stitch on back needle as if to knit, pull yarn through and remove stitch from needle.

Insert tapestry needle into next stitch on back needle as if to purl, pull yarn through, leaving stitch on needle.

Repeat Steps 1 and 2 once.

Step 3

Repeat Step 1.

Step 4

Insert tapestry needle into first stitch on back needle as if to knit, pull yarn through and remove stitch from needle.

Insert tapestry needle into next stitch on back needle as if to knit, pull yarn through, leaving stitch on needle.

Step 5

Repeat Step 1.

Step 6

Insert tapestry needle into first stitch on back needle as if to purl, pull yarn through and remove stitch from needle.

Insert tapestry needle into next stitch on back needle as if to knit, pull yarn through, leaving stitch on needle.

Repeat Steps 5 and 6 until 4 sts remain on each needle; work 3 or 4 stitches at a time, then go back and adjust the tension to match the pieces being joined.

Step 7

Repeat Step 1.

Step 8

Insert tapestry needle into first stitch on back needle as if to purl, pull yarn through and remove stitch from needle.

Insert tapestry needle into next stitch on back needle as if to purl, pull yarn through, leaving stitch on needle.

Repeat Steps 1 and 2 once—1 st remains on each needle.

Final Step

Insert tapestry needle into stitch on front needle as if to knit, pull yarn through and remove stitch from needle.

Insert tapestry needle into remaining stitch as if to knit, pull yarn through and remove stitch from needle.

PATTERN NOTES

You may work Texture Pattern and Right and Left Wedges from text or charts.

Slip the first stitch of every row knitwise with yarn in back. The German Short-Row Double Stitch (DS) is not considered the first st of a row; it should be slipped purlwise with yarn in front.

COWL

Using crochet hook, waste yarn, and Provisional CO, CO 41 sts.

Knit 4 rows, slipping first st of every row knitwise wyib.

Section 1

Work Rows 1–12 of Texture Pattern.

Section 2

Row 1 (RS): Slip 1, knit to end.
Rows 2–5: Repeat Row 1.
Row 6: Slip 1, k2, purl to last 3 sts, k3.
Rows 7 and 8: Repeat Rows 5 and 6.
Rows 9–12: Repeat Row 1.

Section 3

Work Rows 1–14 of Right Wedge.

Section 4

Repeat Section 2.

Section 5

Work Rows 1–15 of Left Wedge.

Section 6

Row 1 (WS): Slip 1, knit to end.
Rows 2–4: Repeat Row 1.
Row 5: Slip 1, k2, purl to last 3 sts, k3.
Row 6 and 7: Repeat Rows 4 and 5.
Rows 8–11: Repeat Row 1.

Repeat Sections 1–6 five more times, ending the final repeat with Row 6 of Section 6. Cut yarn, leaving a tail approximately 40" (101.5 cm) long.

FINISHING

Carefully unravel Provisional CO and place live sts on spare needle, picking up 1 st to return to 41 sts. Using tapestry needle and Kitchener st, graft ends of Cowl together.

Block Cowl as desired.

julie asselin

If you have never encountered a hank of Julie Asselin's hand-dyed yarns, you have been missing out. Brilliantly colored like twists of silk ribbon, glowing from deep within a shelf or standing alone on a web page, her yarns are a riot of unapologetic color. From deep, elephantine grays to fresh, fruity citrus orange, Julie's yarn has gravitational pull in a yarn store—if you sell it, they will come.

French-Canadian by birth, Julie grew up surrounded by craftsmanship and color. Her mother and grandmother, both accomplished seamstresses, knitters, and crafters, shared their knowledge with a young Julie, encouraging her to experiment with textiles, fiber, and natural dyeing. Through exploration of her own concoctions, Julie learned about the colors the world around her could create—and their limitations. She schooled herself in a wide variety of dyeing processes and experimented with them at home, eventually embracing the low-metal, low-impact acid dye method she still uses today.

Julie's initial forays into dyeing yarn created beautiful one-off skeins that she gave to family and friends, and word soon got around in her local community that there was someone dyeing intense, vibrant colors with an artist's eye. Yarn stores reached out, requesting orders, and Julie watched what had been a hobby slowly transform into a business. Conscious of her current wool sources and the potential impact of piecemeal purchasing from larger mills, Julie, along with her husband and business partner, Jean-François, researched local wool producers and mills. They worked to custom-blend yarns to

specifications they knew would create the colors and textures knitters adored. Julie has made sure that throughout the process, her yarns are never from a faceless source, even when they come from other areas of the world.

Several of her yarns are spun from American wools, while others come from expert Merino shepherds in New Zealand. Her superwash process is as low-impact as possible, using a strictly regulated, no-plastic method in Germany that combines salt and carbonization to yield smooth, washable wools. While her yarns may come across continents to arrive in her hands, Julie is careful to organize her shipping routes and methods to be as efficient and low-impact as possible so as not to add damage to the world in her quest for beautiful fiber.

Living just four hours away from Vermont, it was no surprise that eventually she would encounter Green Mountain Spinnery's operation (see page 21). With their values regarding production and sustainability so intensely aligned, Julie was excited at the opportunity to collaborate with the mill on a new project. For a brand built on hand-dyed, pre-spun yarns in small batches, the potential change of process required to produce bales of fibers that could then be carded and spun by the mill's equipment was a new challenge. She and Jean-François devised a way to dye the fluffy scoured fiber in their signature vibrant colors, then worked with Green Mountain Spinnery to combine these dyed fiber batches with the naturally colored sheep fleeces.

Nurtured, the resulting yarn, is a blend of fine wools: Rambouillet, Targhee, and Merino.

It is the perfect marriage of Green Mountain Spinnery's Americana roots and Julie's passion for color and softness. Julie's business has long been based on luxury fibers, and she has proven that even when the fibers are spun more rustically and dyed differently, her values in this aspect have not changed. This yarn is a new side of Julie and Jean-François. Nurtured has all of the coziness we seek from a yarn we already know— it is a cup of tea, a warm fire, and our favorite slippers. Simultaneously, this yarn is new, fresh, and interesting, with a texture that speaks of the natural world and longs to be knit into sweaters we'll pull on for brisk morning walks and long, campfire nights.

While many of Julie's original yarn colors are jewel-like, the blending of cream, gray, and black wools with hand-dyed fiber tempers the color, giving it a range of depth and softness. Saturated flecks concentrate unexpectedly throughout the wool, adding a tweedy, heathered look to each hank. For knitters familiar with the work of Green Mountain Spinnery, Nurtured is a departure from the traditional farm-fresh feel of heritage breeds. For knitters coming from Julie's merino and silk blends, this yarn is a pastoral foray.

The effervescence and joviality of Julie and Jean-François translate into every skein, inviting knitters to try yarn that not only tantalizes but delivers. Much of the beauty of this yarn is in its temporal nature: the color palette changes from year to year, the glossy tones fine-tuned and streamlined with each season. While knitters collect and hoard, Julie and Jean-François are experimenting and editing, thoughtfully taking notes and making tiny changes, striving to communicate who they are through texture, fiber, and color.

Tsuga Cardigan

Designed by Bristol Ivy

Casual and comfortable, this cardigan shrugs on just beside the collarbone, the perfect layer for the first chill of fall air or the last frosty mornings of early spring. Knit from the back yoke out, the construction is approachable for beginner garment knitters and intriguing to experienced crafters. Textured stitches highlight the movement of the draped, open fronts, but are simple enough visually not to distract from the yarn.

The softly heathered Nurtured yarn surprises throughout with flecks of unblended color, even in the soft sand tones of Irma. The cozy, comforting hand of this 100 percent Merino creates a fabric perfect for next-to-skin wear, rendering Tsuga a beautiful, essential addition to your sweater collection.

FINISHED MEASUREMENTS
32 (35, 39, 43, 47, 51, 56, 59)" [81.5 (89, 99, 109, 119.5, 129.5, 142, 150) cm] bust, with fronts open

YARN
Nurtured by Julie Asselin [100% fine wool; 130 yards (119 meters) / 2 ounces (56 grams)]: 8 (8, 9, 10, 11, 12, 13, 14) hanks Irma

NEEDLES
Size US 7 (4.5 mm) circular needle 32" (80 cm) long and needle(s) in your preferred style for working in the rnd

Size US 8 (5 mm) circular needle 32" (80 cm) long and needle(s) in your preferred style for working in the rnd

Change needle size if necessary to obtain correct gauge.

NOTIONS
Stitch markers, including 1 removable marker; stitch holders or waste yarn

GAUGE
16 sts and 26 rows = 4" (10 cm) in St st, using larger needle

16½ sts and 26 rows = 4" (10 cm) in Sand st, using larger needle

17 sts and 26 rows = 4" (10 cm) in Garter Rib, using larger needle

STITCH PATTERNS
GARTER RIB FLAT
(odd number of sts; 2-row repeat)
Row 1 (RS): Knit.
Row 2: P1, *k1, p1; repeat from * to end.
Repeat Rows 1 and 2 for Garter Rib Flat.

GARTER RIB IN RNDS
(even number of sts; 2-rnd repeat)
Rnd 1: Knit.
Rnd 2: *P1, k1; repeat from * to end.
Repeat Rnds 1 and 2 for Garter Rib in Rnds.

SAND STITCH
(odd number of sts; 4-row repeat)
Row 1 (WS): P1, *k1, p1; repeat from * to end.
Row 2: Knit.
Row 3: K1, *p1, k1; repeat from * to end.
Row 4: Knit.
Repeat Rows 1–4 for Sand Stitch.

SPECIAL TECHNIQUE
SSK BO
SSK, *slip 1 knitwise, insert left-hand needle into fronts of last 2 sts on right-hand needle from left to right and knit these 2 sts together through the back loops; repeat from * to end. Fasten off.

PATTERN NOTES
The cardigan is worked in one piece from the top down. The Collar is worked from side to side first and then stitches are picked up along three edges of the Collar. The stitches at each end of the Collar are placed on hold for the Fronts while the remaining stitches along the long edge of the Collar are worked for the Yoke, with shaping for the Sleeves and Back worked along raglan lines. The Sleeve stitches are placed on hold and stitches are picked up along the side edges of the Sleeves for the Fronts, which are then joined to the Back and worked to the bottom edge. The Sleeve stitches are then placed back on the needle(s) and worked from the armhole down to the cuff.

COLLAR

Using smaller 32" (80 cm) long circular needle and Long-Tail CO (see Special Techniques, page 167), CO 3 sts. Begin Garter st; work even for 74 (90, 98, 118, 126, 138, 138, 142) rows [37 (45, 49, 59, 63, 69, 69, 71) Garter ridges], placing a removable marker on the second row to indicate the RS. Do not turn.

YOKE

Rotate work 90 degrees to the right and, using working yarn and needle, pick up and knit 36 (44, 48, 58, 62, 68, 68, 70) sts in side edge (1 st in each Garter ridge except for the first ridge), then rotate work 90 degrees to the right and pick up and knit 3 sts in original CO edge—42 (50, 54, 64, 68, 74, 74, 76) sts.

Next Row (WS): K3 and place these 3 sts on holder or waste yarn for Left Front, p6 (8, 8, 10, 10, 12, 10, 10) for Left Sleeve, pm, p24 (28, 32, 38, 42, 44, 48, 50) for Back, pm, p6 (8, 8, 10, 10, 12, 10, 10) for Right Sleeve, k3 and place these 3 sts on holder or waste yarn for the Right Front—36 (44, 48, 58, 62, 68, 68, 70) sts remain. Do not break yarn.

Shape Yoke

With RS facing, join second ball of yarn. Change to larger 32" (80 cm) long circular needle.

Increase Row 1 (RS): [K1-f/b, knit to 2 sts before marker, k1-f/b, k1, sm] twice, k1-f/b, knit to last 2 sts, k1-f/b, k1—6 sts increased.

Purl 1 row.

Repeat Increase Row 1 every RS row 8 (8, 9, 9, 10, 11, 13, 14) times—90 (98, 108, 118, 128, 140, 152, 160) sts; 42 (46, 52, 58, 64, 68, 76, 80) sts for Back, 24 (26, 28, 30, 32, 36, 38, 40) sts each Sleeve.

Increase Row 2 (RS): Knit to 3 sts before marker, pm, [k1-f/b] twice, k1, sm, k1-f/b, knit to 2 sts before marker, k1-f/b, k1, sm, [k1-f/b] twice, pm, knit to end—96 (104, 114, 124, 134, 146, 158, 166) sts.

Next Row: [Purl to marker, sm, *k1, p1; repeat from * to marker, sm] twice, purl to end.

Increase Row 3 (RS): Knit to 2 sts before marker, pm, [k1-f/b] twice, remove marker, knit to marker, sm, k1-f/b, knit to 2 sts before marker, k1-f/b, k1, sm, knit to marker, remove marker, [k1-f/b] twice, pm, knit to end—6 sts increased.

Next Row: [Purl to marker, sm, *k1, p1; repeat from * to marker, sm] twice, purl to end.

Repeat Increase Row 3 every RS row 9 (10, 11, 12, 13, 15, 16, 17) times (shifting first and last markers 2 sts toward outside edges every RS row)—156 (170, 186, 202, 218, 242, 260, 274) sts; 64 (70, 78, 86, 94, 102, 112, 118) sts for Back, 46 (50, 54, 58, 62, 70, 74, 78) sts each Sleeve.

Next Row (WS): Ssp, work to last 2 sts, p2tog (removing marker)—154 (168, 184, 200, 216, 240, 258, 272) sts remain; 64 (70, 78, 86, 94, 102, 112, 118) sts for Back, 45 (49, 53, 57, 61, 69, 73, 77) sts each Sleeve. Break yarn.

Divide for Body and Sleeves

Division Row (RS): Using yarn attached to 3 sts on hold for Left Front, k3 held sts, pick up and knit 27 (29, 31, 33, 35, 39, 43, 47) sts along side edge of Left Sleeve, place next 45 (49, 53, 57, 61, 69, 73, 77) sts to marker on holder or waste yarn for Left Sleeve, sm, k64 (70, 78, 86, 94, 102, 112, 118) to marker for Back, sm, place next 45 (49, 53, 57, 61, 69, 73, 77) sts to marker on holder or waste yarn for Right Sleeve, pick up and knit 27 (29, 31, 33, 35, 39, 43, 47) sts along side edge of Right Sleeve, k3 sts on hold for Right Front—124 (134, 146, 158, 170, 186, 204, 218) sts.

BODY

Next Row (WS): K3, work Sand st to marker, sm, purl to marker, sm, work Sand st to last 3 sts, k3.

Next Row: K3, work Sand st to marker, sm, knit to marker, sm, work Sand st to last 3 sts, k3.

Work even for 3 rows.

Shape Sides

Increase Row (RS): Work to 1 st before marker, M1R, k1, sm, knit to marker, sm, k1, M1L, work to end—2 sts increased.

Rep Increase Row every 6 rows 15 times, working new sts in Sand st—156 (166, 178, 190, 202, 218, 236, 250) sts.

Work even for 1 row.

Change to smaller 32" (80 cm) long circular needle and Garter st; work even for 8 rows.

BO all sts using Ssk BO.

SLEEVES

Transfer Sleeve sts to larger needle(s) in your preferred style for knitting in the rnd; pm for beginning of rnd. Pick up and knit 1 st from center of underarm; join for working in the rnd—46 (50, 54, 58, 62, 70, 74, 78) sts. Continue Garter Rib as established; work even for 19 (13, 13, 9, 7, 5, 5, 3) rnds.

Shape Sleeve

Decrease Rnd: Ssk, work to last 3 sts, k2tog, p1—2 sts decreased.

Repeat Decrease Rnd every 20 (14, 14, 12, 8, 6, 6, 4) rnds 1 (2, 2, 7, 1, 6, 14, 3) time(s), then every 22 (16, 16, 0, 10, 8, 8, 6) rnds 2 (3, 3, 0, 8, 7, 1, 14) time(s)—38 (38, 42, 42, 42, 42, 42, 42) sts remain. Work even until piece measures 17" (43 cm) from pick-up rnd.

Change to smaller needle(s) in your preferred style for knitting in the rnd.

Next Rnd: Knit the knit sts and purl the purl sts as they face you.

Repeat last rnd for 2" (5 cm). BO all sts using Ssk BO.

FINISHING

Block piece as desired.

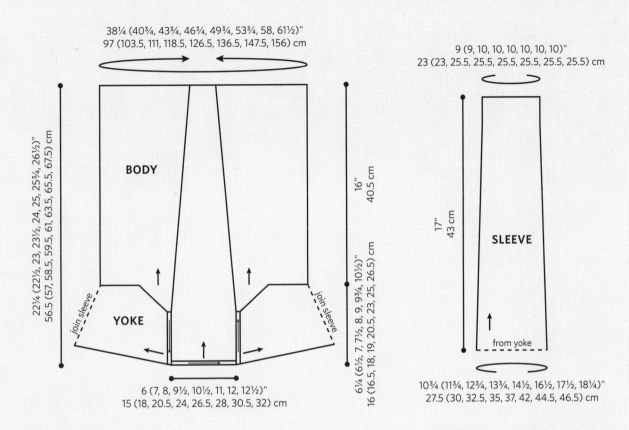

38¼ (40¾, 43¾, 46¾, 49¾, 53¾, 58, 61½)"
97 (103.5, 111, 118.5, 126.5, 136.5, 147.5, 156) cm

9 (9, 10, 10, 10, 10, 10, 10)"
23 (23, 25.5, 25.5, 25.5, 25.5, 25.5, 25.5) cm

BODY

22¼ (22½, 23, 23½, 24, 25, 25¾, 26½)"
56.5 (57, 58.5, 59.5, 61, 63.5, 65.5, 67.5) cm

16"
40.5 cm

17"
43 cm

SLEEVE

join sleeve

YOKE

join sleeve

6¼ (6½, 7, 7½, 8, 9, 9¾, 10½)"
16 (16.5, 18, 19, 20.5, 23, 25, 26.5) cm

from yoke

6 (7, 8, 9½, 10½, 11, 12, 12½)"
15 (18, 20.5, 24, 26.5, 28, 30.5, 32) cm

10¾ (11¾, 12¾, 13¾, 14½, 16½, 17½, 18¼)"
27.5 (30, 32.5, 35, 37, 42, 44.5, 46.5) cm

Note: *Pieces are worked from the top down.*

YARN /for/ THOUGHT

free range

Intrigued by the idea of sourcing carefully? Here are a few more yarns that have been on my knitting wish list—the producers here embody the spirit of careful sourcing, acknowledging and honoring the history of their fiber and sharing it with the end consumer. Transparency helps us make more informed decisions, and for these brands, it is a point of pride. Pick up a skein or two, and see where they take you.

IMPERIAL STOCK RANCH

With a rich history in sustainable practices, this cattle and sheep ranch in Shaniko, Oregon, is a family-owned ranch that has been in operation since 1871. (What could be more idyllic Americana than sheep roaming across open plains, drinking from winding creeks, and grazing alongside elk?) In the 1980s, owner-operator Dan Carver worked with the Natural Resource Conservation Service to develop a plan for the ranch that would continue its sustainable practices and mission into the future. One of my favorite wools from their wool brand Imperial Yarn is Columbia, a bouncy medium-weight wool with lots of character. While not as soft as some other wools, this yarn comes in a palette of beautiful tones just begging to be turned into cozy cabled sweaters.

BEAVERSLIDE DRY GOODS

At the foot of the Rocky Mountains, Beaverslide Dry Goods' 3,000-acre ranch is home to Merino sheep specifically bred and raised to thrive in the harsh and varied conditions of Montana. The owners are passionate about sustainability and have elected to do many tasks the "old-fashioned way," even spinning the wool locally in Alberta, Canada (only a few hours north of the ranch).

Both mill and ranch are conscientious about environmental impact and maintaining the wool's natural character. Every decision made is designed to enhance the feel, wear, and quality of the yarn, which is not carbonized or heavily processed. Beaverslide's 3-ply Heavy Fisherman weight is spun on an 1800s-era spinning mule, resulting in a slightly rustic texture that knits into beautiful garments and accessories.

MALABRIGO YARN

This family-owned and -operated yarn company is based in Montevideo, Uruguay. South America has a rich cultural heritage and history with wool production, continued today by companies like Malabrigo, who work to source fibers for their exquisitely hand-dyed yarns from ranches in Uruguay and Peru. Finito, a 100 percent Merino wool yarn, is a wonderful example of Malabrigo's commitment to use the finest and softest wool available locally. The fiber is available in limited quantity, and Malabrigo has encouraged its production through partnership with SUL (Secretariado Uruguayo de la Lana), an organization dedicated to the development of wool in Uruguay. The resulting wool is cashmere-soft and can be traced back to the individual animals that produce it.

CHAPTER 2

produce

thoughtfully

MODERN CONSUMERS DEMAND ABUNDANCE AND availability: Beneath fluorescent lighting, it is always bountiful summer, with seasonal produce on hand and piled high all year long. Many supermarkets label the origin of our produce, and while some things may travel farther than others, it is not often that you can find locally grown vegetables, fruits, and flowers stocked. While many shoppers will venture to farmers' markets in summer and spring to celebrate the local bounty, these same places tend to fall short when cooler weather approaches—we have become too spoiled by choice to stretch our imaginations by using only what is available around us.

Slow food, a movement focused on using local, high-quality ingredients, has revived the interest in regional culinary tradition. Dandelion greens, wild violets, and heirloom vegetables are raised from humble roots to gourmet plates, and diners are celebrating their inclusion. This movement not only expands our palates and imagination, but also cultivates environmental diversity and stimulates the local economy. By using ingredients produced close to home, restaurants practicing slow food have closer relationships with their communities, in turn sparking relationships between producers and consumers.

While a person exploring slow food might begin cultivation of their own through growing their own vegetables and fruits, it is a bit harder for the individual pursuing slow knitting to start raising sheep. A tomato plant can be grown on a back patio or raised bed garden with a bit of careful effort, but it can take years of knowledge, acres of space, and extensive resources to begin raising livestock successfully with the intent of making beautiful yarn. I find that this is best left to the experts, and instead think that the slow knitting approach to "growing your own" can start with spinning raw fleeces into yarn.

The act of experiencing the process of yarn creation, from shearing to lovingly caressing the fibers into a finished product through spinning, allows us to realize things that we wouldn't have been able to tell just by analyzing premade yarn. When looking at a finished yarn, we rarely get to experience firsthand the length of each fiber or the crimp and sheen of the raw material. Through spinning, we get to not only explore these individual attributes, but also create something new from them. For knitters and fiber lovers who are ambitious and have the space, this process can start with buying a fleece from a county fair. I know many knitters who relish the process of taking home a new fleece to be washed, cleaned, and prepared by hand before spinning. For those of us without the interest or the luxury of space, buying pre-prepared rovings from reputable sources is also a wonderful place to begin the process.

The act of making, in and of itself, is a gift and experience that deepens our understanding of the process and product. Learning how to spin allowed me to form an entirely new relationship with wool. Just as each finished yarn is different, each wool tells a story. As you spin it into yarn, each fleece's properties communicate to you in these moments about how it would like to best become yarn and what type of yarn it would like to become. You can experiment to your heart's content, but generally the fiber itself seems to know if it would like to be nestled against other plies or remain a soft, fussy single, and as you spin, your hands help guide these wishes into a reality.

As a knitter who had never spun before, I knew there were different types of sheep, and that these sheep produced different types of wool. Some wools were rough, and some were soft enough to wear close to your skin. But I would never have seen a difference between Jacob and Columbia, or between Targhee and Rambouillet. Now, having experienced wools in their natural state, I can describe them with adjectives like crunchy, springy, and dense, and terms like micron count, crimp, and hand. How they are spun affects how they will act in the finished project, and the choices are endless. I can choose how the yarn feels—smooth, silky, fluffy, or bouncy—simply by the way that I spin it. By dividing the fiber in different ways, I can dictate whether a finished knit will have strong or subtle striping, bright speckles or muted, slow, gradient changes.

In the same way that chefs can challenge themselves by using only local ingredients, you can challenge yourself by spinning your own wools, even just once. Coarse dual-purpose fleeces can find inspiration in the Icelandic tradition and metamorphose on the wheel into pseudo-Lopi singles, perfect for lightweight and durable outer layers. Fluffy bundles of Texel and Cormo wind up into delightful white skeins that readily soak up color in a dye pot. Deep Moorit fleeces yield heathery, moody yarns that let textured stitches shine.

Knitting with yarns that you have made from the beginning is an incredible process, because you can let the yarn guide you in choosing just the right pattern from the beginning. While the desire to make something perfectly catered to, tailored for, and paired with the garment you have chosen is strong, sometimes the wool has a different idea of what it needs to become. Knitting is a discourse with the character, heritage, and history of a fiber. This will translate into the finished product with a warmth and energy that will far outlast the act of making.

next steps

The idea of producing thoughtfully is about observing and contemplating before creating, about planning your project before you cast on a single stitch. By drawing on history, fine art, fashion, and industry, knitters can relate more wholly to the project and understand what they are making beyond the act of doing so. Making something is about final, tactile satisfaction. Producing thoughtfully explores why we have the drive to do so.

Spinning is a wonderful way to become better acquainted with wool, and it's more accessible than it seems. Those wanting to dip their toes in without a large initial investment can find instructors and materials at many local shops or fiber festivals—I started my own spinning journey with a drop spindle and online videos before graduating to in-person classes and a wheel.

When I began spinning, the first few yarns I produced seemed unworthy of the time spent making them, and certainly not worthy of knitting. Lumpy, bumpy, under or over plied, these yarns had plenty of character, but I found myself spinning with nothing in mind outside of the action of turning wool into yarn. A fine form of meditation, but hardly an acknowledgment of the work required by farmer, sheep, and dyer to get the raw wool into my hands. When I finally worked up the courage to spin for a project in mind, I was astounded by how many of these seeming mistakes worked out in the end garment. Slight variations in weight and texture wet blocked into a single, cohesive fabric that I was proud to wear.

If spinning your own yarn doesn't appeal to you in any way, there are many other ways to explore yarn production and how it pertains to your knitting. Seek out books to explore the cultural knitting heritage of other countries—it is easy to find the yarns mentioned online and experience how they have changed and developed in different ways than where you've learned to knit. Experiment with what is around you just as much as what you order online or buy at a local shop to add diversity and variety to your yarn experiences. By searching these yarns out, you're likely to spend time talking to the people who make them, gaining a better understanding of where you live and what is available in your area. Green thumbs may choose to explore the vast array of natural dyestuffs by cultivating them in an at-home garden, or those who have less luck with plants can experience the beauty of their natural surroundings by learning what may be collected nearby.

brooklyn tweed

Like many who love to knit and read about knitting online, I began following a blog in 2005 called *Brooklyn Tweed*. In digital format, Jared Flood, a young photographer who moved from Tacoma, Washington, to New York, detailed the process of his projects with beautiful photos. He talked about new yarns and shared his appreciation for wool, all while working his way through grad school. Through the blog, Jared developed a following and community of faraway knitters who felt the same way that he did about tweedy, rustic wools. His clear visual style and love of patterns adorned with layers of cables, delicate lace, and traditional shapes quickly made him a sought-after partner for yarn companies, and it wasn't long before he was invited to publish a book of patterns with big-name brand Classic Elite, then creatively helmed by Pam Allen.

Like many who love yarn and knitting, Jared had a sense of how the wool moved from sheep to skein, and he was excited to see more behind the scenes at his first industry show, The National NeedleArts Association's (TNNA) gathering. Eagerly hoping to connect with farmers and mills who had turned their yarns into the wools he loved, Jared was surprised to find that the show floor was instead occupied mostly by brands that sourced wools from far-off mills in Turkey, Italy, Germany, China, and South America. Though there were a few small companies representing the US-grown wool contingency, most yarns being shown represented only the last steps in the yarn-making process.

When Jared was offered the opportunity to design a yarn to coordinate with his brand, he explored the possibility of American-made wool production. Jared and Pam worked together to research the type of yarn he would like to have made, but eventually Jared branched out on his own and visited different mills in New England, finding a common cause with family-owned Harrisville Designs, a century-old woolen mill in New Hampshire.

Harrisville had been producing a line of weaving and knitting yarns for generations and shared Jared's passion for maintaining the American textile industry by expanding their line through his vision. Working in tandem, they educated Jared on the differences in spinning at home and spinning on mill equipment—the changes in terminology, construction, and nuances of sourcing. In his last year of graduate school, he worked on his studies during the day and yarn production on weekends and evenings, graduating and launching his first yarn line, worsted-weight Shelter, in the same year.

The response was insanity. Having never intended to do much more than offer a single yarn for a limited time, Jared and his partners were unprepared for the rush of wholesale and retail orders suddenly flooding them. Yarn stores, excited about the prospect of carrying a Jared Flood yarn line along with the patterns their customers adored, pushed to buy. Without the inventory, Jared spent a good portion of his first year playing catch-up, working with

Harrisville to increase inventory and production and get the yarn into knitters' grasping hands. The company now maintains a steady presence in more than thirty yarn stores and online.

While most companies would branch out to different fibers at this point, Jared continues to offer the American-made Shelter, Loft, Quarry, Arbor, and Plains yarn lines as the staples of the brand. Each is a blend of Targhee- and Columbia-bred fleeces, all sourced in the American West. Jared believes that exploring the facets and possibilities of a single wool is similar to the development of wine. Breeding for wool and blending that wool into a resulting yarn, which is spun slightly differently and at different weights, is as detailed and fine-tuned a process as creating the perfect blend of grapes.

As if making a beautiful yarn wasn't enough, Brooklyn Tweed continues to release beautiful pattern collections in conjunction with the industry's favorite designers. The designs are released throughout the year, and are still fueled by Jared's original vision of simplicity and timelessness combined with historic knitting traditions and values of craftsmanship and utility. The company's recent relocation to Portland, Oregon, was no surprise—the artisan community and wool-friendly weather of the city have already begun to inspire new collections and collaborations under the Brooklyn Tweed label.

Through his careful development, selection, and presentation, Jared Flood has helped revive the world's interest in woolen-spun, American-made wools in a way that only a visionary voice can. His yarns present themselves as simple, hardy creatures that are only what they are—the truest form of wool, striving to be used in the purpose for which they are made.

Grow

Designed by Norah Gaughan

So much more than a cabled pullover, this garment is full of the construction details knitters expect from master designer Norah Gaughan. A pattern of cables reaches from hem to neckline in the heathery greens of Button Jar, much in the way that new plants reach from flat plains to vast skies. With a curved hem and flattering A-line swing shape, this sweater feels feminine over flowy layers, or classic with jeans.

Take your time when knitting with this woolen-spun Shelter yarn from Brooklyn Tweed. Since this yarn is spun to be lofty and light with a warm air-trapping core, pulling too hard can result in a sudden break. This is a project designed to be enjoyed with patience and concentration. Allow yourself to focus on the simple joy of movement and the happiness of moments spent with beautiful wool.

FINISHED MEASUREMENTS
32 (36½, 40, 44½, 48, 51½)" [81.5 (92.5, 101.5, 113, 122, 131) cm] bust

YARN
Brooklyn Tweed Shelter [100% American Targhee-Columbia wool; 140 yards (128 meters) / 1¾ ounces (50 grams)]: 6 (7, 8, 9, 11, 12) skeins Button Jar

NEEDLES
Size US 5 (3.75 mm) circular needles 16" (40 cm) and 32" (80 cm) long

Size US 7 (4.5 cm) circular needle 32" (80 cm) long

Change needle size if necessary to obtain correct gauge.

NOTIONS
Stitch markers in 3 colors; strong yarn in matching weight and color for seams (see Pattern Notes)

GAUGE
18 sts and 28 rows = 4" (10 cm) in St st, using larger needle

41 sts across Charts A, B, and C at bottom edge measures 7½" (19 cm)

79 sts across Charts A, B, C, D, and E at top of Chart B measures 13" (33 cm)

STITCH PATTERNS
2X2 RIB
(multiple of 4 sts + 2; 2-row repeat)
Row 1 (WS): P2, *k2, p2; repeat from * to end.
Row 2: K2, *p2, k2; repeat from * to end.
Repeat Rows 1 and 2 for 2x2 Rib.

1X1 RIB
(even number of sts; 1-rnd repeat)
All Rnds: *K1, p1; repeat from * to end.

PATTERN NOTES
Use Sloped BO (see Special Techniques on page 167) when binding off stitches.

Since woolen-spun yarns like Shelter tend to be delicate for sewing, it is recommended to sew all seams with a strong yarn in a matching color.

SLEEVES

Using smaller needle, CO 34 (38, 38, 42, 42, 46) sts.
Begin 2x2 Rib; work even for 2" (5 cm), ending with a WS row.

Change to larger needle.

Next Row (RS): K2, p2, knit to last 4 sts, p2, k2.

Keeping first and last 4 sts in 2x2 Rib and remaining sts in St st, work even for 9 (9, 3, 7, 3, 3) rows.

Shape Sleeve

Increase Row (RS): K2, p2, M1L, knit to last 4 sts, M1R, p2, k2—2 sts increased.

Repeat Increase Row every 10 (10, 10, 6, 6, 6) rows 7 (7, 6, 2, 7, 6) times, then every 0 (0, 10, 8, 8, 8) rows 0 (0, 3, 8, 5, 6) times—50 (54, 58, 64, 68, 72) sts.

Work even until piece measures 15¾ (16, 16¼, 16½, 16¾, 17)" [40 (40.5, 41.5, 42, 42.5, 43) cm] from the beginning, ending with a WS row.

Shape Cap

BO 3 sts at beginning of next 2 rows, then 2 sts at beginning of next 2 rows, then decrease 1 st each side every RS row 1 (2, 1, 2, 2, 2) time(s), then every 4 rows 6 (6, 7, 7, 7, 8) times, then every RS row 2 (2, 2, 2, 3, 3) times, as follows: K1, k2tog, knit to last 3 sts, ssk, k1. BO 2 sts at beginning of next 2 rows, then 3 sts at beginning of next 2 rows.

BO remaining 12 (14, 18, 22, 24, 26) sts.

BACK

Using smaller needle, CO 32 (44, 48, 60, 64, 76) sts.

Row 1 (WS): P1, work 2x2 Rib to last st, p1.

Rows 2 and 3: Knit the knit sts and purl the purl sts as they face you.

Row 4 (Increase Row): Work 5 sts, M1PR, work to last 5 sts, M1PR, work to end—34 (46, 50, 62, 66, 78) sts.

Rows 5–8: Repeat Rows 1–4—36 (48, 52, 64, 68, 80) sts after Row 8.

Rows 9–11: Repeat Row 2.

Row 12 (Increase Row): Work 5 sts, M1R, work to last 5 sts, M1L, work to end—38 (50, 54, 66, 70, 82) sts.

Rows 13–16: Repeat Rows 9–12—40 (52, 56, 68, 72, 84) sts after Row 16.

Rows 17–19: Repeat Row 2.

Row 20: Change to larger needle. Work 5 sts, M1R, [k5 (8, 5, 7, 8, 6), k2tog] 4 (4, 6, 6, 6, 8) times, knit to last 5 sts, M1L, work to end—38 (50, 52, 64, 68, 78) sts remain.

Working first and last 5 sts in rib as established, and remaining sts in St st, work even for 3 rows.

Shape Sides

Increase Row (RS): Work 5 sts, M1R, knit to last 5 sts, M1L, work to end—2 sts decreased.

Repeat Increase Row every 4 rows 16 (15, 18, 17, 19, 18) times—72 (82, 90, 100, 108, 116) sts.

Work even for 1 row. Piece should measure approximately 12½ (12, 13¾, 13¼, 14¼, 13¾)" [32 (30.5, 35, 33.5, 36, 35) cm] from the beginning.

Shape Armholes

BO 3 sts at beginning of next 2 rows, then 2 sts at beginning of next 2 (4, 4, 8, 8, 12) rows, then decrease 1 st each side every RS row 2 (4, 6, 5, 7, 5) times, as follows: K1, k2tog, knit to last 3 sts, ssk, k1—58 (60, 64, 68, 72, 76) sts remain.

Work even until armholes measure 6½ (7, 7½, 8, 8½, 9)" [16.5 (18, 19, 20.5, 21.5, 23) cm], ending with a WS row. Place marker either side of center 26 (26, 28, 28, 30, 30) sts.

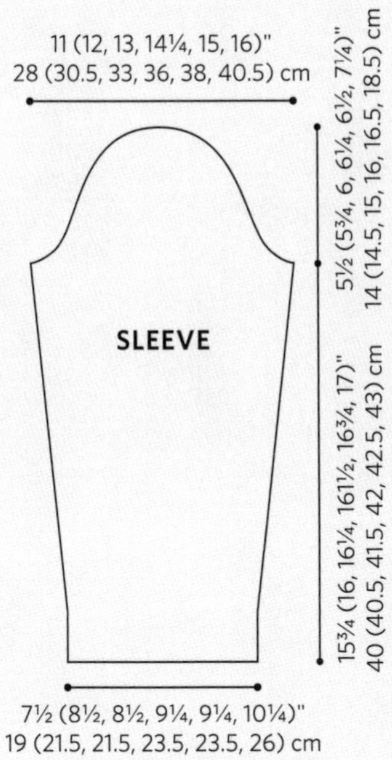
11 (12, 13, 14¼, 15, 16)"
28 (30.5, 33, 36, 38, 40.5) cm
5½ (5¾, 6, 6¼, 6½, 7¼)"
14 (14.5, 15, 16, 16.5, 18.5) cm
SLEEVE
15¾ (16, 16¼, 16½, 16¾, 17)"
40 (40.5, 41.5, 42, 42.5, 43) cm
7½ (8½, 8½, 9¼, 9¼, 10¼)"
19 (21.5, 21.5, 23.5, 23.5, 26) cm

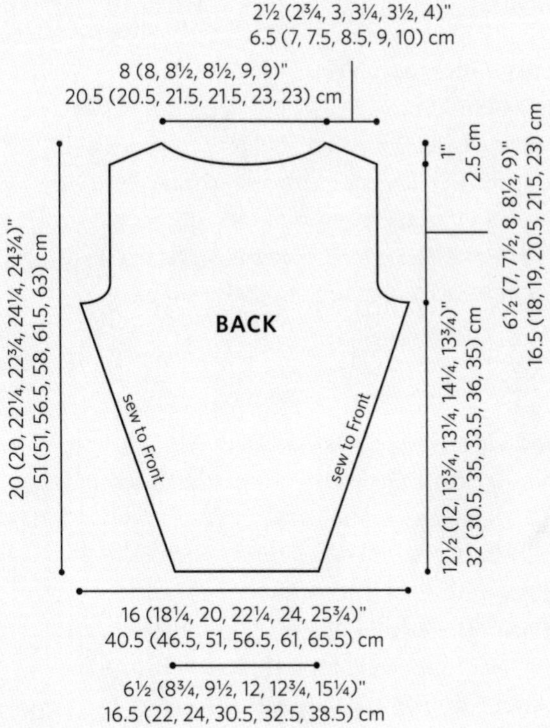
2½ (2¾, 3, 3¼, 3½, 4)"
6.5 (7, 7.5, 8.5, 9, 10) cm
8 (8, 8½, 8½, 9, 9)"
20.5 (20.5, 21.5, 21.5, 23, 23) cm
1"
2.5 cm
6½ (7, 7½, 8, 8½, 9)"
16.5 (18, 19, 20.5, 21.5, 23) cm
20 (20, 22¼, 22¾, 24¼, 24¾)"
51 (51, 56.5, 58, 61.5, 63) cm
BACK
sew to Front
sew to Front
12½ (12, 13¾, 13¼, 14¼, 13¾)"
32 (30.5, 35, 33.5, 36, 35) cm
16 (18¼, 20, 22¼, 24, 25¾)"
40.5 (46.5, 51, 56.5, 61, 65.5) cm
6½ (8¾, 9½, 12, 12¾, 15¼)"
16.5 (22, 24, 30.5, 32.5, 38.5) cm

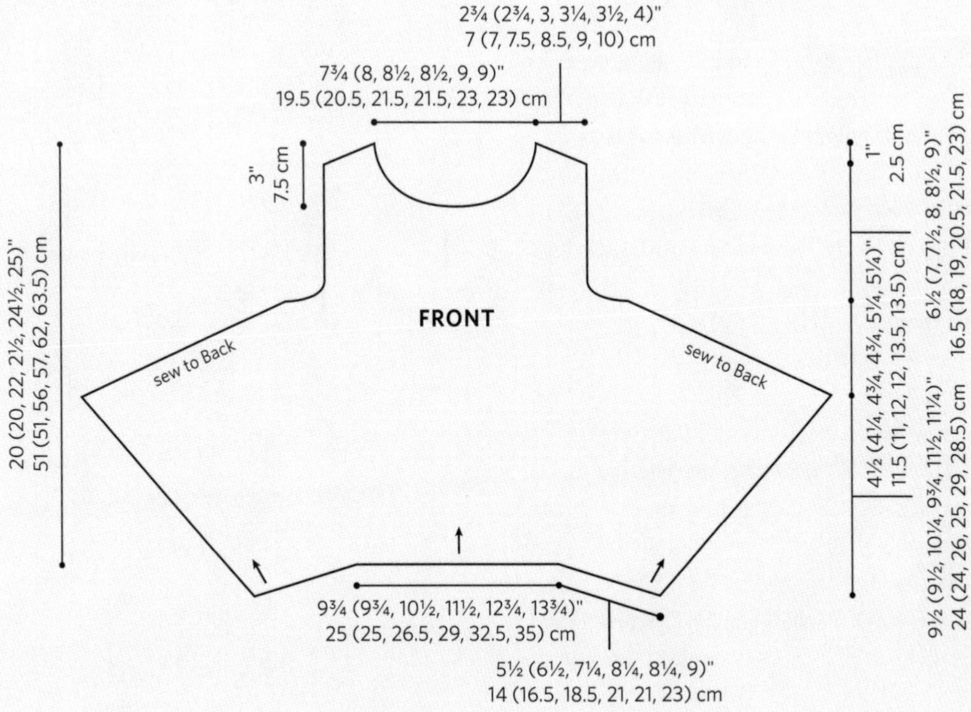
2¾ (2¾, 3, 3¼, 3½, 4)"
7 (7, 7.5, 8.5, 9, 10) cm
7¾ (8, 8½, 8½, 9, 9)"
19.5 (20.5, 21.5, 21.5, 23, 23) cm
3"
7.5 cm
1"
2.5 cm
20 (20, 22, 2½, 24½, 25)"
51 (51, 56, 57, 62, 63.5) cm
FRONT
sew to Back
sew to Back
4½ (4¼, 4¾, 4¾, 5¼, 5¼)"
11.5 (11, 12, 12, 13.5, 13.5) cm
6½ (7, 7½, 8, 8½, 9)"
16.5 (18, 19, 20.5, 21.5, 23) cm
9½ (9½, 10¼, 9¾, 11½, 11¼)"
24 (24, 26, 25, 29, 28.5) cm
9¾ (9¾, 10½, 11½, 12¾, 13¾)"
25 (25, 26.5, 29, 32.5, 35) cm
5½ (6½, 7¼, 8¼, 8¼, 9)"
14 (16.5, 18.5, 21, 21, 23) cm

Shape Shoulders and Neck

Next Row (RS): BO 3 (4, 5, 5, 6, 6) sts, knit to marker, join a second ball of yarn and bind off center sts, knit to end. Working both sides at the same time, BO 3 (4, 5, 5, 6, 6) sts at beginning of next WS row, then 4 (4, 4, 5, 5, 6) sts at each armhole edge twice and, AT THE SAME TIME, BO 5 sts at each neck edge once.

FRONT

Note: You will increase sts within Chart B as you work; while these increased sts will affect the overall st count, they will not be noted below.

Using smaller 32" (80 cm) needle, CO 101 (109, 121, 133, 139, 151) sts.

Row 1 (WS): P3, k2, [p2, k2] 5 (6, 7, 8, 8, 9) times, pm A, p5 (5, 7, 9, 12, 14), pm B, work Chart C across 16 sts, work Chart B across 9 sts, work Chart A across 16 sts, pm B, p5 (5, 7, 9, 12, 14), pm A, [k2, p2] 5 (6, 7, 8, 8, 9) times, k2, p3.

Rows 2 and 3: Knit the knit sts and purl the purl sts as they face you to B marker, sm, work to next B marker, sm, knit the knit sts and purl the purl sts as they face you to end.

Row 4 (Increase Row): Work 5 sts, M1PR, work to last 5 sts, M1PR, work to end—2 sts increased outside of charts.

Row 5: Repeat Row 2.

Row 6 (Increase Row): Repeat Row 4.

Row 7: Repeat Row 2.

Row 8 (Increase Row): Work 5 sts, M1R, work to A marker, M1R, sm, work to next A marker, sm, M1L, sm, work to last 5 sts, M1L, work to end—4 sts increased outside of charts.

Row 9: Repeat Row 2.

Row 10 (Increase Row): Work 5 sts, M1R, work to last 5 sts, M1R, work to end—2 sts increased outside of charts.

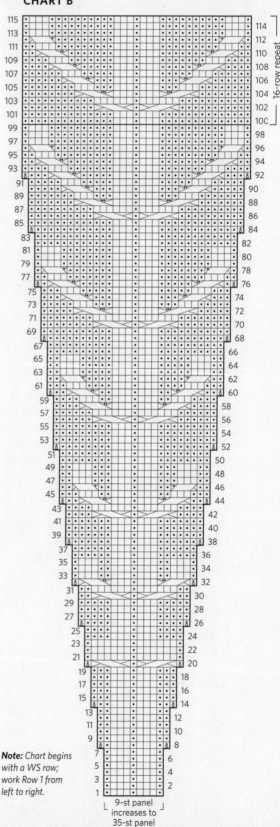

CHART B

16-row repeat

Note: Chart begins with a WS row; work Row 1 from left to right.

9-st panel increases to 35-st panel

CHART A

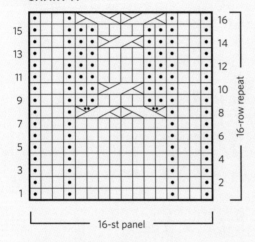

16-row repeat

16-st panel

Note: *Chart begins with a WS row; work Row 1 from left to right.*

CHART C

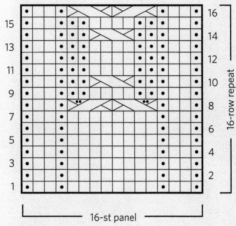

16-row repeat

16-st panel

Note: *Chart begins with a WS row; work Row 1 from left to right.*

CHART D

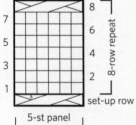

8-row repeat

set-up row

5-st panel increases to 6-st panel

CHART E

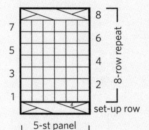

8-row repeat

set-up row

5-st panel increases to 6-st panel

☐   Knit on RS, purl on WS.

•   Purl on RS, knit on WS.

⅄   M1PR

Slip 2 sts to cn, hold to back, k2, k2 from cn.

Slip 2 sts to cn, hold to front, k2, k2 from cn.

Slip 2 sts to cn, hold to back, k2, p2 from cn.

Slip 2 sts to cn, hold to front, p2, k2 from cn.

Slip 1 st to cn, hold to back, k3, p1 from cn.

Slip 3 sts to cn, hold to front, p1, k3 from cn.

Slip 2 sts to cn, hold to back, k3, p2 from cn.

Slip 3 sts to cn, hold to front, p2, k3 from cn.

Slip 2 sts to cn, hold to back, k3, [k1, M1L, k1] from cn.

Slip 3 sts to cn, hold to front, k1, M1L, k1, k3 from cn.

Slip 3 sts to cn, hold to back, k3, k3 from cn.

Slip 3 sts to cn, hold to front, k3, k3 from cn.

Slip 3 sts to cn, hold to back, k3, p3 from cn.

Slip 3 sts to cn, hold to front, p3, k3 from cn.

Row 11: Repeat Row 2.

Row 12 (Increase Row): Repeat Row 4.

Row 13: Repeat Row 2.

Row 14 (Increase Row): Work 5 sts, M1PR, work to 1 st before A marker, M1R, k1, sm, work to next A marker, sm, k1, M1L, work to last 5 sts, M1PL, work to end—4 sts increased outside of charts.

Row 15: Repeat Row 2.

Row 16 (Increase Row): Repeat Row 10.

Rows 17 and 18: Repeat Rows 15 and 16.

Row 19: Repeat Row 2.

Row 20 (Increase Row): Change to larger needle. Work 5 sts, M1R, [k7, k2tog] 3 times, knit to A marker, M1R, sm, work to next A marker, sm, M1L, [k7, k2tog] 3 times, knit to last 5 sts, M1L, work to end—125 (133, 145, 157, 163, 175) sts, including sts increased in chart. Working first and last 5 sts in rib as established, sts between B markers in cable patterns, and remaining sts in St st, work even for 1 row.

Shape Sides, Center, and Armholes

Note: *All shaping (including continued Chart B increases) is worked at the same time through the armhole shaping. Side increases begin first, and then center shaping begins. Once side increases are complete, side BOs begin and are worked to the beginning of the armhole. Center shaping is continued through armhole shaping. At the same time, when piece measures 10" (25.5 cm), an additional cable is added on either side of the center cable panel. Instructions for all of the shaping will be given separately, but will be worked at the same time; please read entire section through before beginning.*

Side Increase Row (RS): Work 5 sts, M1R, work to last 5 sts, M1L, work to end—2 sts increased.

Repeat Side Increase Row every RS row 22 (22, 24, 23, 29, 28) times. Work even for 1 row.

Using Sloped BO, BO 3 sts at beginning of next 2 rows, 4 sts at beginning of next 16 (20, 22, 16, 20, 18) rows, then 3 sts at beginning of next 14 (8, 10, 16, 14, 16) rows. AT THE SAME TIME, beginning on second Side Increase Row, shape center as follows:

Center Increase Row (RS): Work to A marker, M1R, sm, work to next A marker, sm, M1L, work to end—2 sts increased.

Repeat Center Increase Row every 6 rows 3 (3, 10, 2, 1, 1) time(s), then every 8 rows 7 (7, 2, 8, 9, 9) times. AT THE SAME TIME, when piece measures approximately 10" (25.5 cm) from beginning (measured at center Front), begin working new cables as follows:

Set-Up Row (RS): Work to 5 sts before B marker, place new B marker, work Chart D across 5 sts (increasing to 6 sts), remove marker, work to next B marker, remove marker, work Chart E across 5 sts (increasing to 6 sts), place new B marker, work to end. Continue working Charts D and E as established and, AT THE SAME TIME, when side BOs are complete, ending with a WS row, shape armholes as follows:

BO 5 sts at beginning of next 2 rows, 4 sts at beginning of next 2 rows, 2 sts at beginning of next 2 (4, 4, 8, 8, 12) rows, then 1 st at beginning of next 0 (6, 8, 10, 12, 12) rows.

When all shaping is complete, 81 (81, 85, 87, 93, 97) sts remain.

Work even until armholes measure 4½ (5, 5½, 6, 6½, 7)" [11.5 (12.5, 14, 15, 16.5, 18) cm], ending with a WS row. Place marker either side of center 25 (27, 29, 29, 33, 33) sts.

Shape Neck and Shoulders

Note: *Neck and shoulder shaping are worked at the same time; please read entire section through before beginning.*

Next Row (RS): Work to marker, join a second ball of yarn and bind off center sts to next marker (decreasing 6 sts across as you BO to keep edge from flaring), work to end. Working both sides at the same time, BO 4 sts at each neck edge once, 3 sts once, 2 sts once, then 1 st twice. AT THE SAME TIME, when

armholes measure 6½ (7, 7½, 8, 8½, 9)" [16.5 (18, 19, 20.5, 21.5, 23) cm], ending with a WS row, shape shoulders as follows:

Note: *In order to match the st count for the back shoulders, you will decrease sts across the cable sts as you BO.*

BO 5 (6, 5, 6, 7, 7) sts at beginning of next 2 rows, decreasing 2 (0, 0, 1, 0, 0) st(s) over cable sts on each side as you BO; BO 6 (5, 6, 6, 6, 7) sts at beginning of next 2 rows, decreasing 2 (2, 2, 1, 1, 1) st(s) as you BO; BO 6 (5, 6, 6, 6, 7) sts at beginning of next 2 rows, decreasing 2 (2, 2, 1, 2, 2) st(s) as you BO.

FINISHING

Block pieces to measurements. Using strong yarn in similar weight and color to working yarn, sew shoulder seams. Sew BO side edges of Front to side edges of Back (see Schematic). Set in Sleeves. Sew Sleeve seams.

Neckband

Using 16" (40 cm) circular needle, pick up and knit 96 (96, 100, 100, 104, 104) sts around neck edge. Join for working in the rnd; pm for beginning of rnd. Begin 1x1 Rib; work even for ¾" (2 cm). BO all sts in rib.

quince & co.

Open a back issue of *Interweave Knits*, search your shelf of knitting books, or simply glance through your Ravelry library and past projects, and I'm sure you'll find something designed by Quince & Co.'s Pam Allen. From the publication of her first patterns in the early 1980s to her management of one of today's most popular and prolific knitting brands, Pam has been a stable presence in a knitting market that has undergone vast amounts of change.

Pam's earliest published knitting patterns appeared in *Family Circle* magazine. She sustained herself by publishing works and getting herself involved with anything knitting-related, including knitting swatches for yarn companies. She then moved into writing books (like *Knitting for Dummies*, which adorns my own bookshelf and taught me to purl, yarn over, and increase stitches), and she eventually became the editor in chief at *Interweave Knits. Interweave* combined many of Pam's interests—fashion, art, history, research, construction, and instruction—into one neat package. She helped the company weather the industry's move toward new Internet content offerings bolstered by the rise of Ravelry, the popular online knitting and crochet community, and the overnight boom of independent publishing. Afterward, she left *Interweave Knits* to pursue her interest in the making of yarn as creative director at Classic Elite, an established yarn company.

Pam enjoyed the process of coordinating and creating the new visions for each season of yarns, patterns, and campaigns for Classic Elite. During her time there, she got a call from a Texas mohair producer interested in making a yarn featuring his fiber. The fiber was wonderful, but like many large yarn companies, Classic Elite had long forgone using American mills to spin their yarn in favor of better pricing and higher production overseas. Regardless, Pam agreed to see samples. In talking to the mohair farmer, she discovered that a mill local to her in Maine was doing custom spinning, and she decided to do some research. While Classic Elite wasn't interested in expanding to American production at the time, Pam decided to break away and pursue her new dream of becoming a yarn producer with the purpose of rejuvenating American textile production. She partnered with the mill owner, Bob Rice, and launched Quince & Co. in 2010.

Each and every yarn released through Quince & Co. goes through a design process that highlights the unique qualities of the fibers involved. Pam has pulled on her vast experience working with and selecting yarns to create beautiful versions of familiar things. Owl, a worsted-weight, plump two-ply, is one of my favorite examples. Typically, Huacaya alpaca is spun to enhance the slinky, silky aspects of the fiber, resulting in yarns that have great drape, but may be heavy for use in larger garments. Combining alpaca with a special blend of American-bred wool, Owl is then woolen-spun, a method that adds air in between the yarn fibers and allows for warmth that is lofty and lightweight. One of the unique aspects of Owl is that each season,

alpaca colors are slightly different based on the animal's breeding, age, and coloration. This results in a yarn that while not consistent year to year, is truly special in its uniqueness. Instead of seeing this as a challenge, Pam has embraced these differences and introduces new colors of Owl frequently. (Although she does encourage those who knit with this yarn to buy enough for their garment all at once!)

Like the sheep's wool used in Owl, the fiber used in all of Quince & Co.'s yarns is carefully considered and sourced, and not simply in the easiest way possible. After consulting with cotton farmers and discovering that growing and maintaining organic cotton standards wasn't resulting in a premium product, Pam decided to go with Cleaner Cotton™ through the Sustainable Cotton Project. This process uses biologically based processes to manage pests and avoids compounds that create problems for natural wildlife populations, like honeybees. Unlike organic cotton, in which losses and waste create their own harmful results, Cleaner Cotton™ allows farmers to maintain the yields that are

profitable without sacrificing the land's quality and stability.

Six years after its start, Quince & Co. has become synonymous with beautiful, fresh design. Pam Allen has long since bought her partner out and expanded her production from a single mill to five, and has gone from making a handful of yarns to releasing new bases or colors seasonally (the current tally is thirteen yarns). While Quince may still be a fairly small company, Pam hopes it will continue to grow— she never intended it to be a boutique yarn, but instead hopes that someday the company may be large enough to support many farmers. More yarn means more sheep, and more sheep mean more open spaces, ranches, and farms that will not be turned into industrial development or construction. Open space is a commodity that cannot be regained, and Pam is passionate about maintaining as much of it in the United States as possible. Wool, as Pam says, is a living fiber that changes and grows, just like the industry that feeds it.

Sheep Sorrel

Designed by Pam Allen

Who better to design a pattern than the person who designed the yarn? Pam created a simple hat and fingerless mitt set that celebrates the rustic beauty of Owl in high relief. The combination of basic knit and purl stitches used on panels is reminiscent of Guernsey patterning. Ridges of garter stitch and simple cables make these a knit that allows for yarn appreciation throughout the project. Since the stitches are approachable, these make a great group project that knitters of all levels can enjoy.

FINISHED MEASUREMENTS

Hat: 17¼" (44 cm) circumference
Mitts: 7" (18 cm) hand circumference

YARN

Quince & Co. Owl [50% American wool / 50% alpaca; 120 yards (110 meters) / 1¾ ounces (50 grams)]: 3 skeins Mesa (2 skeins for Hat, 1 skein for Mitts)

NEEDLES

Hat: Size US 8 (5 mm) needle(s) in your preferred style for working in the rnd

Mitts: Size US 6 (4 mm) and US 7 (4.5 mm) needle(s) in your preferred style for working in the rnd

Change needle size if necessary to obtain correct gauge.

NOTIONS

Hat: Stitch marker
Mitts: Stitch markers; waste yarn

GAUGE

Hat: 21 sts and 29 rnds = 4" (10 cm) in Hat Pattern, using size US 8 (5 mm) needles

Mitts: 19 sts and 34 rnds = 4" (10 cm) in Garter stitch, using size US 7 (5 mm) needles

SPECIAL ABBREVIATIONS

LT: Slip 1 st to cable needle and hold to front, k1, k1 from cn. To work without a cable needle, insert needle from back to front between first and second sts and knit second st, then knit first st and slip both sts from left needle together.

RT: Slip 1 st to cable needle and hold to back, k1, k1 from cn. To work without a cable needle, skip first st and knit into front of second st, then knit first st and slip both sts from left needle together.

STITCH PATTERNS

HAT PATTERN

(multiple of 15 sts; 4-rnd repeat)
Rnd 1: *P5, k2, p6, k2; repeat from * to end.
Rnd 2: *P1, k3, p1, RT, p1, k4, p1, LT; repeat from * to end.
Rnd 3: *P5, k2, p1, k4, p1, k2; repeat from * to end.
Rnd 4: *P1, k3, p1, RT, p1, k4, p1, LT; repeat from * to end.
Repeat Rnds 1–4 for Hat Pattern.

MITTS PATTERN

(panel of 12 sts; 4-rnd repeat)
Rnd 1: P1, k2, p6, k2, p1.
Rnd 2: P1, RT, p1, k4, p1, LT, p1.
Rnd 3: P1, k2, p1, k4, p1, k2, p1.
Rnd 4: P1, RT, p1, k4, p1, LT, p1.
Repeat Rnds 1–4 for Mitts Pattern.

HAT

Note: Use your preferred method of working in the rnd. Using Long-Tail CO (see Special Techniques, page 167), CO 90 sts. Join for working in the rnd, being careful not to twist sts; pm for beginning of rnd.

Begin Hat Pattern; work even until piece measures 10" from the beginning, ending with Rnd 4 of pattern.

Shape Crown

Rnd 1: *P2tog, p1, p2tog-tbl, k2, p2tog, p2, p2tog-tbl, k2; repeat from * to end—66 sts remain.
Rnd 2: *K3, RT, k4, LT; repeat from * to end.
Rnd 3: *K3tog, [k2tog] 4 times; repeat from * to end—30 sts remain.
Rnd 4: *K2tog; repeat from * to end—15 sts remain.
Cut yarn, leaving a 12" (30.5 cm) tail. Thread tail through remaining sts twice, pull tight, and fasten off.

Finishing

Block as desired.

MITTS

Right Mitt

Note: Use your preferred method of working in the rnd. Using smaller needle(s) and Long-Tail CO (see Special Techniques, page 167), CO 36 sts. Join for working in the rnd, being careful not to twist sts; pm for beginning of rnd.

Rnd 1: P3, work Mitts Pattern over next 12 sts, p3, pm for beginning of palm, p18.
Rnd 2: K3, work to 3 sts before marker, k3, sm, knit to end.
Rnd 3: P3, work to 3 sts before marker, p3, purl to end.
Rnd 4: K3, work to 3 sts before marker, k3, knit to end.
Rnd 5: Repeat Rnd 3.

Change to larger needle.

Rnd 6: Work to marker, sm, k12, k2tog, yo, knit to end.
Rnd 7: Work to marker, sm, purl to end.
Rnd 8: Work to marker, sm, k11, k2tog, yo, knit to end.
Rnd 9: Work to marker, sm, purl to end.
Rnd 10: Work to marker, sm, k10, k2tog, yo, knit to end.
Rnd 11: Work to marker, sm, purl to end.

Shape Thumb Gusset

Rnd 1: Work to marker, sm, k11, yo, knit to end—1 st increased.
Rnd 2: Work to marker, sm, purl to end.
Repeat Rnds 1 and 2 six more times—43 sts; 18 sts for back of hand, 25 sts for palm.

Hand

Next Rnd: Work to marker, sm, k1, place next 11 sts on waste yarn for thumb, CO 4 sts over gap using Backward Loop CO (see Special Techniques, page 167), knit to end—36 sts remain.

Work even until piece measures 6" (15 cm) from the beginning, ending with Rnd 1 of Pattern. BO all sts purlwise.

Thumb

Transfer sts from waste yarn to larger needle(s), pick up and knit 1 st at left side edge of thumb opening, 4 sts from CO sts, then 1 st at right side edge of thumb opening—17 sts. Join for working in the rnd; pm for beginning of rnd.
*Knit 1 rnd. Purl 1 rnd. Repeat from * until thumb measures 1" (2.5 cm) from pick-up rnd, ending with a purl rnd. Bind off all sts purlwise.

Left Mitt

Work as for Right Mitt through Rnd 5.

Change to larger needle.

Rnd 6: Work to marker, sm, k4, yo, ssk, knit to end.
Rnd 7: Work to marker, sm, purl to end.
Rnd 8: Work to marker, sm, k5, yo, ssk, knit to end.
Rnd 9: Work to marker, sm, purl to end.
Rnd 10: Work to marker, sm, k6, yo, ssk, knit to end.
Rnd 11: Work to marker, sm, purl to end.

Shape Thumb Gusset

Rnd 1: Work to marker, sm, k7, yo, knit to end—37 sts.
Rnd 2: Work to marker, sm, purl to end.

Rnd 3: Work to marker, sm, knit to last 11 sts, yo, knit to end—1 st increased.
Rnd 4: Work to marker, sm, purl to end.
Repeat Rnds 3 and 4 five more times—43 sts; 18 sts for back of hand, 25 sts for palm.

Hand

Next Rnd: Work to marker, sm, k13, place next 11 sts on waste yarn for thumb, CO 4 sts over gap using Backward Loop CO, k1—36 sts remain.

Complete as for Right Mitt.

Finishing

Block as desired.

YARN /for/ THOUGHT

handmade

If many of these small-scale wool producers had listened to the ultra-soft wool craze of the early twenty-first century, they might have stopped raising the sheep they loved and were excited about. What a loss that would have been! Learning to embrace the inherent character of a wool leads us one step closer to using it properly and effectively. With the advent of small-scale mill processing and the resurgence of interest in heritage wool breeds, it's only natural that more knitters are looking for wools right under their noses, in their own flocks and farms. These yarns are all produced by people who worked to develop beautiful, unusual wool breeds and turned them into the yarns they dreamed of. Try your hand at using a few to create your own thoughtfully produced garments.

LITTLE GREY SHEEP

This family-owned farm breeds a special blend of Gotland and Shetland sheep for their resulting trademarked British Fine Stein Wool®. Sheared once a year to get the finest wool and spun in Devon, this yarn is then returned to the farm and hand dyed into a stunning array of kettle-dyed and painted colors. The 4-ply fingering weight comes in smaller skein sizes ideal for colorwork or larger skein sizes for accessories and garments.

DOC MASON

Doc Mason's small herd of Clun Forest and Cheviot sheep have duties far beyond growing their wooly coats. Doc Mason lives in the hills of New Hampshire, where he works as a veterinarian rehabilitating working sheep dogs. The wool is gathered by Ellen Odacier, who numbers the clip annually and has it spun on nearby Prince Edward Island, where some fluffy Maritime wool is added to meet the requirement for a full machine run. The wool is available dyed in a range of colors with delightful names like Unripe Banana and Brakelight. Hefty, sturdy, and squishy, these skeins are for rustic-wool lovers, but are approachable to all when knit into warm mittens with delicately soft linings.

STARCROFT FIBER NASH ISLAND LIGHT

This 100 percent Maine Island organic wool yarn has an interesting history. In Maine, there is a long-standing tradition of using the uninhabited islands off the coast to raise hearty sheep breeds. The Circone family raised sheep on Little Nash Island and Big Nash Island for nearly a hundred years before passing the herd to Jenny Circone's next-door neighbors and close friends, the Wakemans, who still tend this small herd of 150 sheep. The sheep remain wild, grazing the islands. During lambing and shearing seasons, the Wakemans work with the family that owns Starcroft Fiber Mill to gather up the fleeces and bring them by boat to the mainland, where they are turned into skeins and hand-dyed in small batches. Nash Island Light, a worsted-weight yarn produced by Starcroft, is the first I added to my own stash—the fog-washed, delicate tonality of each hand-dyed colorway showcases stitches beautifully.

CHAPTER 3

think
environmentally

EMBRACING THE SEASONALITY OF OUR craft is as much a part of slow knitting as anything else. As the availability of our materials changes throughout the year, so does our role as knitters. Working in harmony with the seasonal cycle helps us feel our place in nature's ebb and flow. Spring and summer teach us to collect and explore the bounty of what is around us and to prepare for the turn indoors in fall and winter, where we will set ourselves about keeping warm and making use of what we have gathered. In the end, it all comes down to working with nature, plant or animal.

In autumn, crafters make pilgrimage en masse to fiber festivals and wool shops to stock up for winter projects. This is the best time of year to be a knitter—the leaves are changing and the warmth of late-year sunshine softens the chilly, damp breath of winter. Woolen things of past years make their way back into our wardrobes, pulled out of storage to warm fingers and toes, and as we gather them up we revive our memories of their making. New knitters are born, in yarn shops or the homes of friends, where they will learn the ritual of beginning.

If fall is our origin season, winter is the apex. We comfort ourselves and those around us by gathering in warmly lit rooms, picking up knitting and nesting in deep, cozy afghans and handmade pullovers. Southern winters are short and kind, while their Northern cousins are cold and indifferent. This indifference somehow makes you heartier, as if the cold reminds you that you are a tender, living being. These true winters can reach deep into your bones and rattle them; each breath yields a startling sensation of *living*. Some part of me always misses the chill of the Midwestern winters of Iowa. Although I've relocated, I still sniff the air on the coldest days to see if snow is coming (you can tell by the lack of humidity and the stillness). I love seeing fat, fluffy flakes falling outside while I sit in a favorite chair with my wheel whirring or needles clicking.

Spring and summer bring with them new growth and welcome us outside. Oppressive heat tends to settle in Tennessee, my current home, during the summer months, making knitting uncomfortable without the aid of air conditioning. I have heard and said many times that the warmer seasons are for smaller projects, like blanket squares, socks, and baby things, but the truth is that summer is for being outdoors to explore and renew our souls through sunshine, glittering water, and deep woods. While I cannot imagine putting down my knitting for half of the year, I find that my knitting bookends my day rather than engulfs it—I plod along on existing projects as the mood strikes.

It is important, as a slow knitter, to embrace this seasonal change and celebrate rather than fight it. These months give me time to dream about the projects I want to begin and start seeking out their materials. The onslaught of warmer weather is not a knitting down season, but a season of inspiration. This turn outdoors allows us to explore our craft in a new way, to delve into the abundance of nature, and to prepare our stock for the later portion of the year. I seek to memorize the colors in tiny blooms and magnificent sunsets and store them for later use in projects that will bring me a breath of life in the cold, echoing winter.

It is through this exploration of abundance that textile lovers in centuries past discovered the world of natural dyeing. The idea of going out and collecting natural dyestuffs each season is enchanting—what a perfect way to extend our love of textiles into warmer months while also experiencing nature fully. Through the exploration and study of plants and natural dyes, we gain a deeper understanding of the world around us and what it has to offer. The materials and cast-offs from our kitchens and gardens can be used to create a dazzling array of color for our knitted creations, from humble onion skins to marigolds. Frequently in these warm months, mason jars find themselves seated on my windowsill, yarn floating within like anatomical specimens suspended in hues of amber.

The best part of working with naturally dyed fibers is the feeling that comes with starting a project in yarn with so many facets. With naturally dyed wools, sometimes I even take the time to wind the ball painstakingly by hand, placing the prized skein in a deep, hand-thrown ceramic yarn bowl, and really absorb myself in the initial cast-on. Using wooden needles somehow completes the effect, helping me reach back through the collective textile history of people doing the same thing, so many years ago, and hoping for the same results—beautiful, wearable garments that keep me warm in fall and winter until the spring blooms again.

There are many people who have made natural dyeing the center of their craft, producing beautiful, naturally dyed yarns and fabrics that any can appreciate and take home. With a better understanding of what they are doing, we come armed to the yarn store or festival stand, ready to appreciate the unusual green, the deep indigo blue, the cochineal magenta, because we know the story of how they came to be. While it may not be feasible to add a full selection of mordants, alums, apothecary jars, and cauldrons to your own worldly possessions, it is always possible to appreciate what the environment around us provides and to eagerly await the next season for all that it brings.

next steps

Explore the seasonality of your knitting by reflecting on the transition from fleece to yarn. Animals are shorn around the time the weather turns warm—this is the perfect time of year to shed your own wooly coats, cardigans, and sweaters. While fleeces are cleaned and prepared for milling and market, knitters' beloved garments can be examined, repaired, washed, and stored for their next use.

Whirring machinery transforms the raw material into yarn, while knitters translate the abundant beauty of the season into inspiration and motivation. This is a time for anticipation and excitement, record-keeping and taking stock. Summer is a wonderful time to cull unwanted yarns from your stash and unravel projects that have gone astray, making room for those to come.

Autumn is breeding season for sheep; they will spend the winter months developing not only wooly coats but also new lambs for spring. The first breaths of cool air in autumn are a missive to knitters everywhere: Gather up what you will need for winter, cast on new projects, and turn the skeins on your shelves into serviceable woolens. Cold weather is coming!

Winter is a time of closeness—livestock clustered in barns gather warmth from those around them. Knitters do much the same, sending loved ones out in the world each day, embracing them in wooly layers of mittens, hats, socks, and scarves. This is a time of celebration and enjoyment, of slowing down and savoring. We draw out the garments of previous years, gathering them around us as we gather our friends and family close. The appreciation we have for these people and materials, this process, will drive us to cast on new things. What we make will become necessary components of the next cycle's passing.

bare naked wools

In interviewing and doing the research surrounding this book, I was continually humbled by the makers who know so much about animal fibers and by all of the discoveries and notes they had made during the process of making and creating beautiful yarns. Such is the case with Anne Hanson of Bare Naked Wools—I left our conversation feeling that this was someone who truly, deeply, and intimately knew fiber.

Anyone who knits most likely knows of Anne Hanson. She has published more than 400 individual patterns, teaches routinely at knitting events around the globe, and started a yarn club before subscriptions were as commonplace as they are now. While I had heard of Anne, I had not had the pleasure of speaking to her or encountering her yarns before the Indie Untangled Rhinebeck Trunk Show, which takes place the weekend of the New York State Sheep & Wool Festival in Rhinebeck, New York (a mecca for fiber artists, truly). While the trunk show floor was dominated by an array of beautifully hand-dyed yarns in vibrant colors, the booth for Anne's company, Bare Naked Wools, stood out, a resting place for the eye with its soft, natural tones of cream, gray, brown, and black. Anne sits among the yarns and embodies them perfectly: at first she seems small and unassuming, but upon closer inspection you discover that there is so much more to her than meets the eye. Years of knitting experience and textile knowledge culminated in her collection of truly versatile and diverse wool yarns that captivate those who use them.

The first unique feature of Bare Naked Wools is that all of the yarns are only available in their natural colors. Anne has coaxed into being dozens of yarns that embrace the inherent qualities of their materials in the purest form—they are unaltered by any method other than blending naturally colored fibers with other plant and animal fibers. The end goal of these yarns is to produce handmade textiles worthy of labor-intensive handknit garments.

For Anne, it is second nature to return to think of fabrics as the first part of the knitting experience. A tailor and professional pattern drafter by trade, she worked from 1981 to 1997 for several fashion houses. She began selling knitting patterns on a local level, then quickly adapted to the Internet market, becoming one of the first knitwear designers to sell patterns on her website and through Ravelry. Before the rise of the web, knitwear designers had to rely heavily on being published or on teaching to stay current and be seen. With the newfound rise of Internet sales, the market became wide open; no restrictions on publication meant that Anne could create the patterns she wanted and sell them directly to the customers who wanted them most.

While working at a yarn store in Ohio, Anne was asked by the owner to learn how to spin yarns in order to teach spinning to interested students. She quickly fell in love with the act of handling raw fibers and turning them into custom yarns. She discovered not only the differences in wool breeds, but also that dyeing and coloring

rovings and finished yarns resulted in a loss of character in the finished wools. She decided to experiment by taking what she had learned as a designer and combining it with her spinning knowledge, and she worked with a textile mill to produce the first ever Knitspot club yarn in 2012.

The sock yarn from this line, called Breakfast Blend, was well received. She released the yarn again as a DK (double knitting yarn) in the Knitspot shop and discovered how wide the audience was for what she was making. What had started as a small side project had quickly evolved—one batch of wool, one color, and Breakfast Blend had started Bare Naked Wools. Addicted to engineering yarns from scratch, she moved on to play with additional fibers, both plant and animal. Bare Naked Wools, dedicated to providing naturally colored yarns that celebrate the qualities of their included fibers, seems so simple at face value, but has a core as complex and carefully considered as architecture.

Stone Soup DK was one of the early yarns for Bare Naked Wools. At spinning mills, it is common for there to be "leftovers"—bits and pieces left over from whole lots of fiber sent by farmers or producers and then left to the mill. Often, these leftovers fall from the carding machines and can be gathered up later and spun into seconds or mill end yarns. Anne saw potential in these mixed bags of bits. Inspired by the parable of Stone Soup, in which a roaming traveler encourages others to create a stew by each donating one item to the pot, thus resulting in a delicious meal for all, Anne sought to blend these yarns together in a way that would create a yarn unique unto itself. Bits of alpaca, silk, and wool combined to create a nubbly, highly textured yarn spun for balance and upcycled from what would have been lost. Warm without heaviness, Stone Soup DK creates a lofty, lightweight fiber that results in some of Anne's most livable garments.

Bare Naked Wools follows a simple principle: The wool knows best. The resilience and qualities of an excellent animal combined with centuries of selective breeding have created a material that can be trusted to do any number of jobs. Anne's yarns are about allowing the wool to speak for itself in the most natural, environmental way possible, which in turn removes the elements that distract most knitters from truly getting to know their wools. By carefully selecting the spin and structure of each yarn, Anne identifies and highlights the fleece's characteristics and purpose. Crimp, elasticity, sheen, a soft hand or durability; each is celebrated for exactly what it is. When we trust materials to be what they are and embrace them for how they behave, we get a yarn that is so much bigger than the sum of its parts.

Wild Grains

Designed by Jennifer Wood

The parable of Stone Soup comes into play when knitting with Bare Naked Wools' yarn of the same name—a handful of textured stitches and a bit of winding cable are combined to make a hearty garment that will keep the wearer occupied with making during the warmer months and cozy during the cooler ones. This shawl collar cardigan encourages knitters to gather up their skills and put them to use, with fresh construction that gives the look of a set-in sleeve without additional seaming. The heathered, rich brown of this blended fiber adds a second level of warm richness to this ambitious layering piece.

SIZES
To fit bust sizes 30-32 (33-35, 36-38, 39-41, 42-44, 45-47, 48-50, 51-53, 54-56, 57-59, 60-62)" [76-81.5 (84-89, 91.5-96.5, 99-104, 106.5-112, 114.5-119.5, 122-127, 129.5-134.5, 137-142, 145-150, 152.5-157.5) cm]

FINISHED MEASUREMENTS
31½ (35, 38, 41½, 44½, 48¼, 52½, 55½, 59¾, 64¼, 67¾)" [80 (89, 96.5, 105.5, 113, 122.5, 133.5, 141, 152, 163, 172) cm] bust, with fronts overlapped

YARN
Bare Naked Wools Stone Soup DK [80% wool / 15% alpaca and llama / 5% combination of tencel, bamboo, silk, and bison; 300 yards (275 meters) / 4 ounces (115 grams)]: 7 (7, 8, 8, 9, 9, 10, 11, 11, 12, 12) hanks Marble

NEEDLES
Size US 4 (3.5 mm) circular needle 32" (80 cm) long and needle(s) in your preferred style for working in the rnd

Change needle size if necessary to obtain correct gauge.

NOTIONS
Crochet hook size US E-4 (3.5 mm) for Provisional CO; waste yarn; stitch markers in two separate colors (color A to mark charts, color B to separate pieces); removable stitch markers; stitch holders; cable needle

GAUGE
22 sts and 28 rows = 4" (10 cm) in St st

74-st Back Chart = 10¼" (26 cm) wide

STITCH PATTERNS
SEED STITCH FLAT
(even number of sts; 1-row repeat)
Row 1 (RS): *P1, k1; repeat from * to end.
Row 2: Knit the purl sts and purl the knit sts as they face you.
Repeat Row 2 for Seed Stitch Flat.

SEED STITCH IN THE RND
(odd number of sts; 1-rnd repeat)
Rnd 1: K1, *p1, k1; repeat from * to end of rnd.
Rnd 2: Knit the purl sts and purl the knit sts as they face you.
Repeat Rnd 2 for Seed Stitch in the Rnd.

SPECIAL TECHNIQUES
CABLE CO
Make a loop (using a slip knot) with the working yarn and place it on the left-hand needle (first st CO), knit into slip knot, draw up a loop but do not drop st from left-hand needle; place new loop on left-hand needle; *insert the tip of the right-hand needle into the space between the last 2 sts on the left-hand needle and draw up a loop; place the loop on the left-hand needle. Repeat from * for remaining sts to be CO, or for casting on at the end of a row in progress.

PROVISIONAL (CROCHET CHAIN) CO
Using a crochet hook and smooth yarn (crochet cotton or ravel cord used for machine knitting), work a crochet chain with a few more chains than the number of sts needed; fasten off. If desired, tie a knot on the fastened-off end to mark the end that you will be unraveling from later. Turn the chain over; with working needle and yarn, starting a few chains in from the beginning of the chain, pick up and knit one st in each bump at the back of the chain, leaving any extra chains at the end unworked.

When ready to work the live sts, unravel the chain by loosening the fastened-off end and unzipping the chain, placing the live sts on a spare needle.

SHORT ROW SHAPING

Work the number of sts specified in the instructions, wrap and turn (w&t) as follows:

To wrap a knit st, with yarn in back, slip the next st purlwise to the right-hand needle, bring yarn to the front, return the slipped st on the right-hand needle to the left-hand needle purlwise; turn, ready to work the next row, leaving the remaining sts unworked.

To wrap a purl st, work as for wrapping a knit st, but begin with the yarn to the front (purl position) before slipping the st, and bring it to the back after slipping the st.

When short rows are completed, or when working progressively longer short rows, work the wrap together with the wrapped st as you come to it as follows:

If st is to be worked as a knit st, insert the right-hand needle into the wrap, from below, then into the wrapped st; k2tog; if st to be worked is a purl st, insert needle into the wrapped st, then down into the wrap; p2tog. (Wrap may be lifted onto the left-hand needle, then worked together with the wrapped st if this is easier.)

PATTERN NOTES

This Cardigan is worked in one piece from the top down. The Collar is worked in two halves from a Provisional CO, then placed on hold. The Saddles are picked up from the inside edges of the Collar, worked for the width of the shoulders, then placed on hold. Stitches for the Back are picked up from the side edges of the Saddles and the inside edge of the Collar, worked through short-row shoulder shaping and armhole edge shaping, then placed on hold. Stitches for the Fronts are picked up from the front side edge of the Saddles, worked with the Collar for a short distance, including short-row shoulder shaping and armhole edge shaping, then placed on hold. The Fronts and Back are joined for the Yoke and stitches are picked up along the sides of the Front and Back for the Sleeves. The Yoke is worked to the base of the armholes, where the Sleeve stitches are placed on hold while the Body is worked to the bottom edge. The bottom edge is finished with a Knit-On Border. The Sleeve stitches are placed back on the needles and worked to the bottom edge.

When working charts, if you do not have enough stitches to work a complete cable, work the affected sts as they appear.

When working short-row shaping for the Collar, it is not necessary to work the wraps together with the wrapped stitches; the Seed stitch pattern will hide them. When working the shoulders, you will need to work the wraps together with the wrapped stitches.

COLLAR

Right Half

Using crochet hook, waste yarn, and Provisional CO, CO 31 (31, 31, 37, 37, 37, 43, 43, 43, 43, 43) sts.

Row 1 (RS): P1, work 20 (20, 20, 26, 26, 26, 32, 32, 32, 32, 32) sts in Seed st, k1, pm color A, work Right Collar Chart to end. Place removable marker to indicate RS of Collar; leave marker in place until sts have been picked up for Back.

Note: *When Cardigan is worn, Collar will be folded over so that WS of Collar is facing.*

Row 2: Work to marker, sm, k1, work in Seed st to last st, k1.

Shape Collar

Note: *Collar is shaped using short rows. Do not work wraps together with wrapped sts as you come to them.*

Set-Up Row (RS): Work to end.

Rows 1 and 2: Work to end.

Short Row 3: Work to marker, sm, k1, work 14 sts, w&t.

Short Row 4: Work to end.

Short Row 5: Work to marker, sm, k1, work 6 sts, w&t.

Short Row 6: Work to end.

Repeat Rows 1–6 four (4, 4, 4, 4, 4, 5, 5, 5, 5) times, then repeat Rows 1 and 2 once.

Repeat Rows 1–6 five (5, 5, 5, 5, 5, 5, 6, 6, 6, 6) times, then repeat Rows 1 and 2 once.

Repeat Rows 1–6 two (2, 2, 2, 3, 3, 3, 3, 3, 3, 3) times, then repeat Row 1 once.

Break yarn and place sts and marker on holder or waste yarn, making note of last chart row worked.

Left Half

With RS of Right Collar facing, carefully unravel Provisional CO and place sts on needle, picking up 1 additional st to return to original st count.

Row 1 (RS): Work Left Collar Chart across 9 sts, pm color A, k1, work in Seed st to last st, p1.

Row 2: K1, work in Seed st to 1 st before marker, k1, sm, work to end.

Shape Collar

Note: *Do not work wraps together with wrapped sts as you come to them.*

Row 1 (RS): Work in established patterns to end.

Row 2: Work to end.

Short Row 3: Work to marker, sm, k1, work 14 sts, w&t.

Short Row 4: Work to end.

Short Row 5: Work to marker, sm, k1, work 6 sts, w&t.

Short Row 6: Work to end.

Repeat Rows 1–6 four (4, 4, 4, 4, 4, 4, 5, 5, 5, 5) times, then repeat Rows 1 and 2 once.

Repeat Rows 1–6 five (5, 5, 5, 5, 5, 5, 6, 6, 6, 6) times, then repeat Rows 1 and 2 once.

Repeat Rows 1–6 two (2, 2, 2, 3, 3, 3, 3, 3, 3, 3) times, then repeat Rows 1 and 2 once.

Break yarn and place sts and marker on holder or waste yarn; Left Half should end with same chart row as Right Half. Place removable markers along inside (shorter) edge of Collar, ½" in from each end.

RIGHT SADDLE

With RS of Collar facing, beginning at left marker, pick up and knit 6 sts along inside edge between marker and held Collar sts.

Set-Up Row (WS): Work Saddle Chart across 6 sts.

Work even until piece measures 4 (4¼, 4¼, 4½, 4½, 4½, 4¾, 4¾, 5, 5, 5)" [10 (11, 11, 11.5, 11.5, 11.5, 12, 12, 12.5, 12.5, 12.5) cm] from pick-up row, ending with a WS row. Break yarn and place sts on holder or waste yarn, making note of last chart row worked.

LEFT SADDLE

With RS of Collar facing, beginning at opposite end of Collar, pick up and knit 6 sts along inside edge between held Collar sts and right marker. Complete as for Right Saddle, ending with same chart row.

BACK

With RS of Left Saddle facing, using circular needle, pick up and knit 26 (27, 27, 28, 28, 28, 29, 30, 30, 31, 31) sts evenly along left edge of Left Saddle between held Left Saddle sts and inside edge of Collar, 46 (48, 50, 50, 52, 54, 54, 56, 58, 58, 58) sts evenly along inside edge of Collar to base of Right Saddle, then 26 (27, 27, 28, 28, 28, 29, 30, 30, 31, 31) sts evenly along right edge of Right Saddle to held Saddle sts—98 (102, 104, 106, 108, 110, 112, 116, 118, 120, 120) sts.

Shape Shoulders

Note: Shoulders are shaped using short rows. Work wraps together with wrapped sts as you come to them.
Set-Up Row (WS): P12 (14, 15, 16, 17, 18, 19, 21, 22, 23, 23), pm color A, work Back Chart across 74 sts, pm color A, purl to end.
Short Rows 1 and 2: Working sts on either side of Back Chart in St st, work to last 13 (15, 16, 17, 18, 15, 15, 17, 18, 19, 19) sts, w&t.
Short Row 3: Work to 4 (4, 4, 5, 5, 4, 4, 5, 5, 5, 5) sts past wrapped st from previous RS row, w&t.
Short Row 4: Work to 4 (4, 4, 5, 5, 4, 4, 5, 5, 5, 5) sts past wrapped st from previous WS row, w&t.
Short Rows 5 and 6: Repeat Short Rows 3 and 4.
Short Row 7: Work to end.
Work even until you have completed Row 24 of Back Chart. Break yarn and place sts on holder or waste yarn.

RIGHT FRONT

With RS of Right Saddle facing, pick up and knit 29 (31, 31, 33, 34, 34, 35, 36, 37, 37, 37) sts evenly along left edge of Right Saddle between held Right Saddle sts and held Right Collar sts, work in established patterns across 31 (31, 31, 37, 37, 37, 43, 43, 43, 43, 43) Right Collar sts—60 (62, 62, 70, 71, 71, 78, 79, 80, 80, 80) sts.

Shape Shoulder

Note: Work wraps together with wrapped sts as you come to them.
Set-Up Row (WS): Work 30 (30, 30, 36, 36, 36, 42, 42, 42, 42, 42) sts, pm color A, work Right Front Cable Chart to last 2 sts, beginning and ending as indicated in chart, pm color A, p2.
Row 1: K2, sm, work to end.
Short Row 2: Work to first marker, work 8 (8, 8, 8, 8, 8, 11, 11, 11, 11, 11) sts, w&t.
Short Row 3: Work to end.
Short Row 4: Work to 8 (8, 8, 8, 8, 8, 7, 7, 12, 12, 12) sts past wrapped st from previous WS row, w&t.
Short Row 5: Work to end.
Short Row 6: Work to 7 (7, 7, 8, 8, 8, 6, 6, 6, 6, 6) sts past wrapped st from previous WS row, w&t.
Short Row 7: Work to end.
Row 8: Work to end.

Shape Front

Increase Row (RS): K2, sm, M1R (or M1PR to keep in pattern), work to end—1 st increased.
Repeat Increase Row every RS row 7 times, working new sts into Right Front Cable, and ending with Row 8 of chart—68 (70, 70, 78, 79, 79, 86, 87, 88, 88, 88) sts. Break yarn and place sts and markers on holder or waste yarn.

BACK CHART

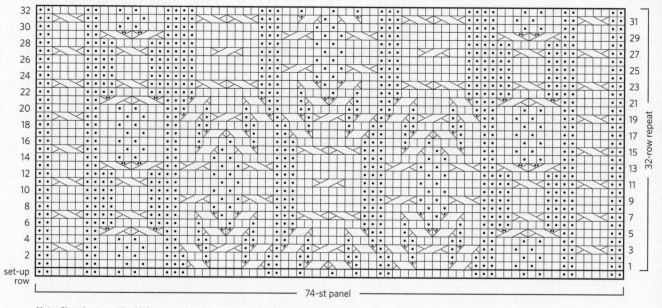

set-up row

74-st panel

Note: Chart begins with a WS row; work set-up row from left to right.

SADDLE CHART

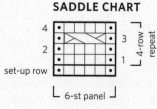

set-up row

4-row repeat

6-st panel

Note: Chart begins with a WS row; work set-up row from left to right.

RIGHT COLLAR CHART

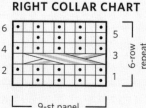

6-row repeat

9-st panel

LEFT COLLAR CHART

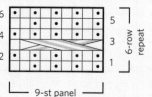

6-row repeat

9-st panel

SLEEVE CHART

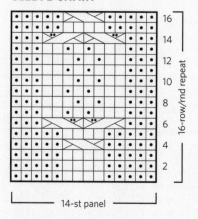

14-st panel

16-row/rnd repeat

Note: Chart begins with a WS row; work Row 1 from left to right.

Knit on RS, purl on WS.

Purl on RS, knit on WS.

Slip 1 st to cn, hold to back, k2, p1 from cn.

Slip 2 sts to cn, hold to front, p1, k2 from cn.

Slip 2 sts to cn, hold to back, k2, k2 from cn.

Slip 2 sts to cn, hold to front, k2, k2 from cn.

Slip 2 sts to cn, hold to back, k2, p2 from cn.

Slip 2 sts to cn, hold to front, p2, k2 from cn.

Slip 4 sts to cn, hold to front, [k1, p1] twice, [k1, p1] twice from cn.

Slip 4 sts to cn, hold to front, [p1, k1] twice, [p1, k1] twice from cn.

RIGHT FRONT CABLE CHART

set-up row

16-row repeat

7-st repeat

beg all sizes

end sizes 31½ and 55½"
end sizes 59¾, 64¼, and 67¾"
end sizes 35 and 38"
end size 41½"
end sizes 44½ and 48¼"
end size 52½"

Note: *Chart begins with a WS row; work set-up row from left to right.*

LEFT FRONT CABLE CHART

set-up row

16-row repeat

7-st repeat

beg size 52½"
beg sizes 44½ and 48¼"
beg size 41½"
beg sizes 35 and 38"
beg sizes 59¾, 64¼, and 67¾"
beg sizes 31½ and 55½"

end all sizes

Note: *Chart begins with a WS row; work set-up row from left to right.*

LEFT FRONT

Transfer 31 (31, 31, 37, 37, 37, 43, 43, 43, 43, 43) Left Collar sts and marker to circular needle. With RS facing, work across these sts in established patterns to last st, pm color A, p1, pick up and knit 29 (31, 31, 33, 34, 34, 35, 36, 37, 37, 37) sts evenly along right edge of Left Saddle to held Left Saddle sts—60 (62, 62, 70, 71, 71, 78, 79, 80, 80, 80) sts.

Shape Shoulder

Note: Work wraps together with wrapped sts as you come to them.

Set-Up Row (WS): P2, pm color A, work Left Front Cable Chart to marker A, beginning and ending as indicated in chart, sm, work to end.

Short Row 1: Work to first marker, sm, work 8 (8, 8, 8, 8, 8, 11, 11, 11, 11, 11) sts, w&t.

Row 2: Work to end.

Short Row 3: Work to 8 (8, 8, 8, 8, 8, 7, 7, 12, 12, 12) sts past wrapped st from previous RS row, w&t.

Short Row 4: Work to end.

Short Row 5: Work to 7 (7, 7, 8, 8, 8, 6, 6, 6, 6, 6) sts past wrapped st from previous RS row, w&t.

Short Row 6: Work to end.

Note: For sizes 44½, 48¼, 52½, 55½, and 59¾", do not work last cable crossing on Row 7 of chart; work affected sts in St st instead.

Row 7: Work to end.

Row 8: Work to end.

Shape Front

Increase Row (RS): Work to last 2 sts, M1L (or M1PL to keep in pattern), sm, k2—1 st increased.

Repeat Increase Row every RS row 7 times, ending with Row 8 of chart—68 (70, 70, 78, 79, 79, 86, 87, 88, 88, 88) sts.

YOKE

With RS facing, transfer all held sts and markers to circular needle so that they are in the following order, from right to left: Left Front, Left Saddle, Back, Right Saddle, and Right Front—246 (254, 256, 274, 278, 280, 296, 302, 306, 308, 308) sts.

Begin Sleeves

With RS facing, continuing in patterns as established, work across Left Front to last 2 sts, M1L (or M1PL to keep in pattern), sm, k2, pm color B for Left Sleeve, pick up and knit 16 sts evenly along side edge of Left Front to Saddle sts, work across Saddle sts (making note of Saddle Chart row worked), pick up and knit 16 sts evenly along side edge of Back, pm color B for end of Left Sleeve, work across 98 (102, 104, 106, 108, 110, 112, 116, 118, 120, 120) Back sts, pm color B for Right Sleeve, pick up and knit 16 sts evenly along side edge of Back to Saddle sts, work across Saddle sts, pick up and knit 16 sts evenly along side edge of Right Front, pm color B for end of Sleeve, k2, sm, M1R (or M1PR to keep in pattern), work to end—312 (320, 322, 340, 344, 346, 362, 368, 372, 374, 374) sts; 69 (71, 71, 79, 80, 80, 87, 88, 89, 89, 89) sts each Front, 38 sts each Sleeve, and 98 (102, 104, 106, 108, 110, 112, 116, 118, 120, 120) sts for Back.

Set-Up Row (WS): [Work to B marker, p12, pm color A, work Sleeve Chart across 14 sts (beginning with Row 3 if last row of Saddle Chart worked was Row 1, or Row 1 of Sleeve Chart if last row of Saddle Chart worked was Row 3), pm color A, purl to B marker, sm] twice, work to end.

Shape Yoke

Front and Sleeve Increase Row (RS): Work to 2 sts before B marker, M1L (or M1PL), k2, sm, RLI, work to next B marker, LLI, sm, work to next B marker, sm, RLI, work to next B marker, LLI, sm, k2, M1R (or M1PR), work to end—6 sts increased.

Repeat Front and Sleeve Increase Row every RS row 12 (12, 12, 11, 11, 10, 8, 9, 6, 4, 3) times—390 (398, 400, 412, 416, 412, 416, 428, 414, 404, 398) sts; 82 (84, 84, 91, 92, 91, 96, 98, 96, 94, 93) sts each Front, 64 (64, 64, 62, 62, 60, 56, 58, 52, 48, 46) sts each Sleeve, and 98 (102, 104, 106, 108, 110, 112, 116, 118, 120, 120) sts for Back.

Body and Sleeve Increase Row (RS): Work to 2 sts before B marker, M1L (or M1PL), k2, sm, RLI, work to next B marker, LLI, sm, k1, RLI, work to 1 st before next B marker, LLI, k1, sm, RLI, work to next B marker, LLI, sm, k2, M1R (or M1PR), work to end—8 sts increased.

Repeat Body and Sleeve Increase Row every RS row 0 (1, 1, 3, 4, 7, 10, 12, 17, 21, 23) time(s)—398 (414, 416, 444, 456, 476, 504, 532, 558, 580, 590) sts; 83 (86, 86, 95, 97, 99, 107, 111, 114, 116, 117) sts each Front, 66 (68, 68, 70, 72, 76, 78, 84, 88, 92, 94) sts each Sleeve, and 100 (106, 108, 114, 118, 126, 134, 142, 154, 164, 168) sts for Back.

Work even for 1 row.

Divide Body and Sleeves

Dividing Row (RS): Removing original B markers as you come to them, work to 2 sts before B marker, sm, k2, place next 66 (68, 68, 70, 72, 76, 78, 84, 88, 92, 94) sts on holder or waste yarn for Left Sleeve, CO 4 (7, 14, 17, 21, 24, 27, 28, 28, 30, 35) sts for underarm, work 100 (106, 108, 114, 118, 126, 134, 142, 154, 164, 168) Back sts, place next 66 (68, 68, 70, 72, 76, 78, 84, 88, 92, 94) sts on holder or waste yarn for Right Sleeve, CO 4 (7, 14, 17, 21, 24, 27, 28, 28, 30, 35) sts for underarm, k2, sm, work to end—274 (292, 308, 338, 354, 372, 402, 420, 438, 456, 472) sts.

BODY

Continuing in patterns as established and working CO underarm sts in St st, work even for 1 row.

Shape Collar and Fronts

Note: Collar and Fronts are shaped at the same time; please read entire section through before beginning.

Collar Decrease Row (RS): Work to first marker (at end of Left Collar Chart), sm, k2tog, work to 2 sts before last marker (at beginning of Right Collar Chart), ssk, sm, work to end—2 sts decreased.

Repeat Collar Decrease Row every 4 rows 1 (1, 1, 17, 17, 17, 28, 28, 28, 28, 28) time(s), then every 6 rows 18 (18, 18, 8, 8, 8, 3, 3, 3, 3, 3) times. AT THE SAME TIME, beginning on first Collar Decrease Row, shape Fronts as follows:

Front Increase Row (RS): Work to third marker, M1L (or M1PL), sm, work to third marker from end, sm, M1R (or M1PR), work to end—2 sts increased.

Repeat Front Increase Row every 4 rows 33 (33, 33, 33, 34, 34, 34, 35, 35, 35, 35) times, working increased sts into Front Charts—302 (320, 336, 354, 372, 390, 408, 428, 446, 464, 480) sts; 10 Collar sts and 87 (90, 90, 93, 96, 98, 100, 105, 108, 110, 111) Front sts.

Work even through Row 4 or 6 of Collar Charts.

Piece should measure approximately 19½ (19½, 19½, 19½, 20, 20, 20, 20½, 20½, 20½, 20½)" [49.5 (49.5, 49.5, 49.5, 51, 51, 51, 52, 52, 52, 52) cm] from underarm.

Knit-On Border

With RS facing, using Cable CO, CO 7 sts. Working across sts just CO, k1, [k1-f/b] 4 times, p1, k1, turn—11 Border sts.

Set-Up Row (WS): P1, k1, sm, work Left Collar Chart to end, beginning with Row 2.

Row 1: Work Collar Chart, p1, ssk (last Border st together with 1 Collar st), turn.

Row 2: Slip 2 sts from right-hand needle back to left-hand needle, sssp (last Border st together with 2 Collar sts), k1, work to end.

Row 3: Work Collar Chart, p1, sssk (last Border st together with 2 Collar sts), turn.

Rows 4 and 5: Repeat Rows 2 and 3.

Note: Continue to work across bottom edge of Body, joining 1 Border st to 1 Body st as you go. Work Joining to Cable Panels when working across Front Cable Charts and Back Chart; work Joining to Stockinette when working across St st sections. At end of Right Front Cable Chart, end with a RS row, then proceed to Joining to Right Collar. You will not necessarily begin each new section with a RS row; be sure to work the appropriate row for the side of the work that you are on.

Joining to Cable Panels

Note: If the last row worked was a WS row, begin with Row 1 below; if it was a RS row, begin with Row 2.

Row 1 (RS): Work Collar Chart, p1, ssk (last Border st together with 1 Body sts, turn.

Row 2: Slip 1 st from right-hand needle back to left-hand needle, ssp, k1, work to end.

Repeat Rows 1 and 2 to join to cable panels.

Joining to Stockinette

Note: If the last row worked was a WS row, begin with Row 1 below; if it was a RS row, begin with Row 2.

Row 1 (RS): Work Collar Chart, p1, ssk (last Border st together with 1 Body st), turn.

Row 2: Slip 1 st from right-hand needle to left-hand needle, ssp (last Border st together with 1 Body st), k1, work to end.

Row 3: Repeat Row 1.

Row 4: Slip 1 st wyif from left-hand needle to right-hand needle, k1, work to end.

Repeat Rows 1–4 to join to St st section.

Joining to Right Collar

Row 1 (WS): Slip 2 sts from right-hand needle to left-hand needle, sssp (last Border st together with 2 Collar sts), k1, work to end.

Row 2: Work Collar Chart, p1, sssk (last Border st together with 2 Collar sts), turn.

Rows 3 and 4: Repeat Rows 1 and 2.

Row 5: Slip last st from right-hand needle to left-hand needle, ssp (last Border st together with 1 Collar st), k1, work to end.

Row 6: Work Collar Chart, p1, k1, turn.

BO Row: BO 1 st, [k2tog, BO last st worked] 4 times, k1, BO last st worked. Fasten off.

SLEEVES

With RS of Body facing, using needle(s) in your preferred style for knitting in the rnd, and beginning at center of sts CO for underarm, pick up and knit 2 (4, 7, 9, 11, 12, 13, 14, 14, 15, 18) sts evenly along CO edge, work in established pattern across 66 (68, 68, 70, 72, 76, 78, 84, 88, 92, 94) held Sleeve sts, pick up and knit 2 (3, 7, 8, 10, 12, 14, 14, 14, 15, 17) sts evenly along remaining CO edge to center of underarm—70 (75, 82, 87, 93, 100, 105, 112, 116, 122, 129) sts. Join for working in the rnd; pm for beginning of rnd. Work even for 14 (11, 8, 8, 6, 5, 5, 4, 4, 4, 3) rnds, working sts on either side of Sleeve Cable in St st.

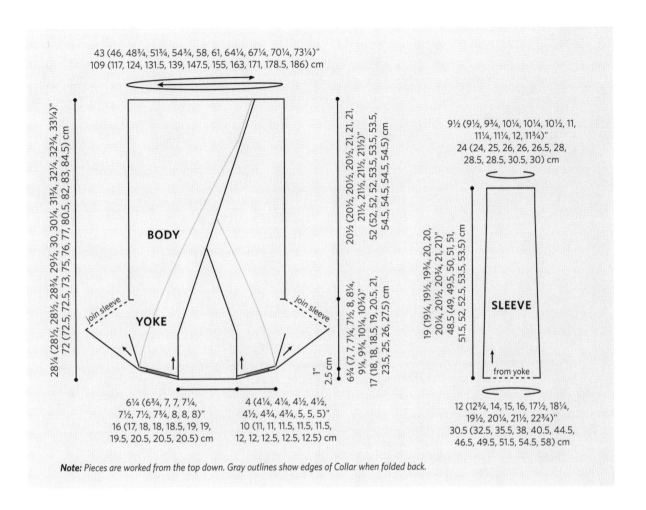

43 (46, 48¾, 51¾, 54¾, 58, 61, 64¼, 67¼, 70¼, 73¼)"
109 (117, 124, 131.5, 139, 147.5, 155, 163, 171, 178.5, 186) cm

9½ (9½, 9¾, 10¼, 10¼, 10½, 11, 11¼, 11¼, 12, 11¾)"
24 (24, 25, 26, 26, 26.5, 28, 28.5, 28.5, 30.5, 30) cm

28¼ (28½, 28½, 28¾, 29½, 30, 30¼, 31¾, 32¼, 32¾, 33¼)" cm
72 (72.5, 72.5, 73, 75, 76, 77, 80.5, 82, 83, 84.5) cm

BODY

YOKE

join sleeve   join sleeve

20½ (20½, 20½, 20½, 21, 21, 21, 21½, 21½, 21½, 21½)"
52 (52, 52, 52, 53.5, 53.5, 53.5, 54.5, 54.5, 54.5, 54.5) cm

6¾ (7, 7, 7¼, 7½, 8, 8¼, 9¼, 9¾, 10¼, 10¾)"
17 (18, 18, 18.5, 19, 20.5, 21, 23.5, 25, 26, 27.5) cm

19 (19¼, 19½, 19¾, 20, 20, 20¼, 20½, 20¾, 21, 21)"
48.5 (49, 49.5, 50, 51, 51, 51.5, 52, 52.5, 53.5, 53.5) cm

SLEEVE

from yoke

1"
2.5 cm

6¼ (6¾, 7, 7, 7¼, 7½, 7½, 7¾, 8, 8, 8)"
16 (17, 18, 18, 18.5, 19, 19, 19.5, 20.5, 20.5, 20.5) cm

4 (4¼, 4¼, 4½, 4½, 4½, 4¾, 4¾, 5, 5, 5)"
10 (11, 11, 11.5, 11.5, 11.5, 12, 12, 12.5, 12.5, 12.5) cm

12 (12¾, 14, 15, 16, 17½, 18¼, 19½, 20¼, 21½, 22¾)"
30.5 (32.5, 35.5, 38, 40.5, 44.5, 46.5, 49.5, 51.5, 54.5, 58) cm

Note: Pieces are worked from the top down. Gray outlines show edges of Collar when folded back.

Shape Sleeve

Decrease Rnd: K1, k2tog, work to last 3 (2, 3, 2, 2, 3, 2, 3, 3, 3, 2) sts, ssk, k1 (0, 1, 0, 0, 1, 0, 1, 1, 1, 0)—2 sts decreased.

Repeat Decrease Rnd every 15 (12, 9, 9, 7, 6, 6, 5, 5, 5, 4) rnds 2 (3, 8, 2, 11, 12, 9, 19, 13, 10, 24) times, then every 14 (11, 8, 8, 6, 5, 5, 4, 4, 4, 3) rnds 4 (5, 3, 10, 4, 6, 10, 3, 11, 15, 5) times—56 (57, 58, 61, 61, 62, 65, 66, 66, 70, 69) sts rem.

Work even until piece measures 16 (16¼, 16½, 16¾, 17, 17, 17¼, 17½, 17¾, 18, 18)" [40.5 (41.5, 42, 42.5, 43, 43, 44, 44.5, 45, 45.5, 45.5) cm] from underarm, or to 3" (7.5 cm) less than desired length.

Next Rnd: Work to marker decreasing 2 (2, 2, 3, 3, 3, 2, 2, 2, 3, 3) sts evenly spaced to marker, remove marker, decrease 5 (4, 5, 4, 4, 5, 4, 5, 5, 5, 4) sts in pattern to next marker, remove marker, work to end decreasing 2 (2, 2, 3, 3, 3, 2, 2, 2, 3, 3) sts evenly spaced to end—47 (49, 49, 51, 51, 51, 57, 57, 57, 59, 59) sts remain.

Work in Seed st for 3" (7.5 cm). BO all sts loosely in pattern.

sincere sheep

Dyeing with natural materials is a great way to stay in touch with the seasonality of your projects, but it requires much more than a keen knowledge of plants. Natural dyeing requires experience with mordants, alums, and measurements, temperature changes and detailed record keeping—it's part chemistry, part history, and part practical magic. It's amazing to me that anyone could become a single repository for the vast amount of knowledge involved with the process, especially on the scale required for yarn sales. When I brought this up while talking to Brooke Sinnes, founder of Sincere Sheep (and natural yarn dyer extraordinaire), she pointed out the simple truth that the vast research needed for natural dyeing has been done over the course of human history. Someone else has already made the mistakes, recorded the results, and laid the foundation for those who are doing it now to expand upon.

This history of natural dyes is fascinating. Seemingly simple elements of the natural world—tiny flowers, small leafy greens, even small insects—had the power in early human history to change the course of trade routes, influence international commerce, and determine the success or failure of expeditions to new lands. Cochineal, a tiny insect that feeds off particular cacti in the Americas, helped reshape the look of European textiles in the 1500s. One color produced is responsible for the British military's iconic red coats. Now, Brooke uses this color to get beautiful deep reds and purples for her yarns, among the veritable rainbow of other shades she

acquires through the use of materials with an equally interesting history.

Brooke's interest in natural dyeing began when she was learning to spin. As part of the learning process, her spinning teacher required her to dye her handspun yarns with natural dyes. Any botanist will tell you that planting a seed in fertile ground is likely to grow a plant, and for Brooke, this experience was a seed of interest that grew into a business. She began dyeing at home for her own personal enjoyment and expanded to sourcing, dyeing, and selling wools under her own label.

One of her favorite things about naturally dyed yarns is how they look good on many people as garments—colors from the natural world often combine more readily with a range of skin tones and complexions. She enjoys not only the history of the dyes, but the modern businesses they support and the ecology that is the result of natural dyes. Plants grown by farmers for dyestuffs help sustain different methods of agriculture around the world, encouraging environmental consciousness in their communities. If natural dyeing can be a successful business, it's less likely that factory farms and large-scale production will transform the places where these plants grow naturally. (Sincere Sheep's yarns are predominantly dyed with plant materials, although Brooke does use insects from time to time.)

Brooke's driving principle is *terroir*—a term used by wine growers around her in California's Napa Valley to describe a wine that is produced

within a single, complete, natural environment. The yarn lines at Sincere Sheep tend to focus on single-breed wools, sourced and spun locally on the West Coast when possible. Rambouillet, Polwarth, and Cormo all play a role in the squishy, vibrant skeins that Brooke displays at shows and fiber festivals, and certainly attract crafters of all varieties.

One of the things that I personally love about Brooke's wool is how some of the spins are more rustic than others—the Rambouillet, in particular, has a wonderful nubby hand similar to my handspun at home. Cormo, which is Julia Farwell-Clay's favorite (and used in her pattern on page 94), is the epitome of squishy softness. None of Brooke's yarns have the limp, lifeless quality often seen in commercially sourced yarns, and that has gained her a loyal following among designers and everyday knitters alike. Using a yarn that embodies and communicates the environment in which it was conceived is almost like taking a journey to that place yourself. Brooke is our Northern California travel guide, mapping the topography of her region for us with plants, color, and fiber.

Russian Sage

Designed by Julia Farwell-Clay

Natural dyeing can resemble alchemy: The dyer puts a bit of wood, foliage, or powder into the dyepot and hours (occasionally days) later, yarn emerges in a color that may be entirely dissimilar to the tone of the natural substance used. Julia Farwell-Clay's pullover has lace stitches that behave much the same way, with loops and directed stitches altered to reveal dropped columns that flank lengthy floral motifs. Naturally dyed Cormo wool in soft violet-gray tones from Sincere Sheep adds extra elasticity and bounce to every stitch. This sweater can be knit to a larger size for a roomy, oversized look, or kept close fitting with negative ease for that classic, New England shape.

SIZES
Small (Medium, Large, 1X-Large, 2X-Large, 3X-Large)

To fit bust sizes 30-32 (34-36, 38-40, 42-44, 46-48, 50-52)" [76-81.5 (86.5-91.5, 96.5-101.5, 106.5-112, 117-122, 127-132) cm]

FINISHED MEASUREMENTS
33½ (37½, 41½, 45½, 49½, 53½)" [85 (95.5, 105.5, 115.5, 125.5, 136) cm] bust

YARN
Sincere Sheep Cormo Sport [100% domestic Cormo wool; 400 yards (366 meters) / 4 ounces (114 grams)]: 4 (5, 5, 6, 6, 7) skeins Winter's Night

NEEDLES
Size US 7 (4.5 mm) circular needle 32" (80 cm) long and needle(s) in your preferred style for working in the rnd

Size US 6 (4 mm) circular needle 32" (80 cm) long and needle(s) in your preferred style for working in the rnd

Change needle size if necessary to obtain correct gauge.

NOTIONS
Stitch markers; stitch holders or waste yarn; cable needle; tapestry needle

GAUGE
24 sts and 32 rows = 4" (10 cm) in St st, using larger needles

38 sts in Wave Lace measures 7" (18 cm) wide

SPECIAL ABBREVIATIONS
C6B: Slip 3 sts to cn, hold to back, k3, k3 from cn.
C6F: Slip 3 sts to cn, hold to front, k3, k3 from cn.

STITCH PATTERNS
WAVE LACE (see Chart)
(multiple of 7 sts + 3; 10-rnd repeat)
Rnd 1: *K4, k2tog, k1, yo; repeat from * to last 3 sts, k3.
Rnd 2: *K3, k2tog, k2, yo; repeat from * to last 3 sts, k3.
Rnd 3: *K2, k2tog, k3, yo; repeat from * to last 3 sts, k3.
Rnd 4: *K1, k2tog, k4, yo; repeat from * to last 3 sts, k3.

Rnd 5: *K2tog, k5, yo; repeat from * to last 3 sts, k3.
Rnd 6: K3, *yo, k1, ssk, k4; repeat from * to end.
Rnd 7: K3, *yo, k2, ssk, k3; repeat from * to end.
Rnd 8: K3, *yo, k3, ssk, k2; repeat from * to end.
Rnd 9: K3, *yo, k4, ssk, k1; repeat from * to end.
Rnd 10: K3, *yo, k5, ssk; repeat from * to end.
Repeat Rnds 1–10 for Wave Lace.

BODY CABLE (see Chart)
(panel of 19 sts; 12-rnd repeat)
Rnds 1 and 3: Yo, k2tog, p1, ssk, yo, k9, yo, k2tog, p1, ssk, yo.
Rnd 2 and all Even-Numbered Rnds: Knit.
Rnd 5: Yo, k2tog, p1, ssk, yo, C6B, k3, yo, k2tog, p1, ssk, yo.
Rnds 7 and 9: Repeat Rnd 1.
Rnd 11: Yo, k2tog, p1, ssk, yo, k3, C6F, yo, k2tog, p1, ssk, yo.
Rnd 12: Repeat Rnd 2.
Repeat Rnds 1–12 for Body Cable.

BODY CABLE

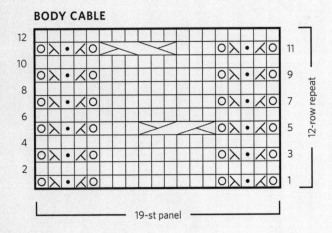

19-st panel

12-row repeat

WAVE LACE

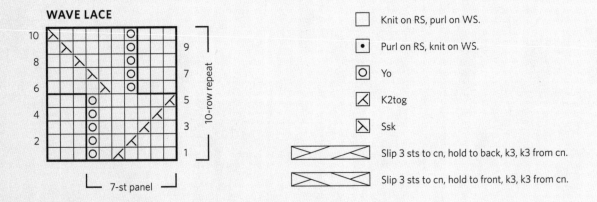

7-st panel

10-row repeat

☐ Knit on RS, purl on WS.

• Purl on RS, knit on WS.

O Yo

K2tog

Ssk

Slip 3 sts to cn, hold to back, k3, k3 from cn.

Slip 3 sts to cn, hold to front, k3, k3 from cn.

SLEEVE CABLE

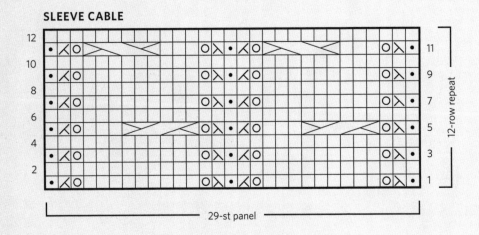

29-st panel

12-row repeat

SLEEVE CABLE (see Chart)

(panel of 29 sts; 12-rnd repeat)

Rnds 1 and 3: [P1, ssk, yo, k9, yo, k2tog] twice, p1.

Rnd 2 and all Even-Numbered Rnds: Knit.

Rnd 5: [P1, ssk, yo, C6B, k3, yo, k2tog] twice, p1.

Rnds 7 and 9: Repeat Rnd 1.

Rnd 11: [P1, ssk, yo, k3, C6F, yo, k2tog] twice, p1.

Rnd 12: Repeat Rnd 2.

Repeat Rnds 1–12 for Cable Eyelet.

SPECIAL TECHNIQUE
KITCHENER STITCH

Using a blunt tapestry needle, thread a length of yarn approximately 4 times the length of the section to be joined. Hold the pieces to be joined wrong sides together, with the needles holding the sts parallel, both ends pointing to the right. Working from right to left, insert tapestry needle into first st on front needle as if to purl, pull yarn through, leaving st on needle; insert tapestry needle into first st on back needle as if to knit, pull yarn through, leaving st on needle; *insert tapestry needle into first st on front needle as if to knit, pull yarn through, remove st from needle; insert tapestry needle into next st on front needle as if to purl, pull yarn through, leave st on needle; insert tapestry needle into first st on back needle as if to purl, pull yarn through, remove st from needle; insert tapestry needle into next st on back needle as if to knit, pull yarn through, leave st on needle. Repeat from *, working 3 or 4 sts at a time, then go back and adjust tension to match the pieces being joined. When 1 st remains on each needle, cut yarn and pass through last 2 sts to fasten off.

PATTERN NOTES

Front and Back hems are worked separately for 2" and 2½" (5 and 6.5 cm), respectively, then joined for the Body. Body and Sleeves are worked separately in the round from the bottom to the underarms, then joined for the Yoke, which is worked in the round to the neck, with raglan shaping. The back neck is shaped using short rows.

When working raglan shaping, do not work a yo in pattern without a corresponding decrease, and vice versa; work affected st(s) in St st.

When working short-row shaping, you may find that the st that you are to wrap is a yo or a st involved in a decrease. If this should happen, work one st more or less before wrapping.

You may work Wave Lace, Body Cable, and Sleeve Cable from text or charts.

BODY

Front Hem

Using smaller circular needle, CO 94 (110, 126, 142, 158, 174) sts.

Row 1 (RS): K3, [p2, k2] 1 (3, 5, 7, 9, 11) time(s), p2, pm, k2, p1, [k3, p2] twice, k3, p1, k2, pm, [p2, k2] 9 times, p2, pm, k2, p1, [k3, p2] twice, k3, p1, k2, pm, [p2, k2] 2 (4, 6, 8, 10, 12) times, k1.

Row 2: P3, [k2, p2] 1 (3, 5, 7, 9, 11) time(s), k2, sm, p6, k2, p3, k2, p6, [k2, p2] 9 times, k2, p6, k2, p3, k2, p6, sm, [k2, p2] 2 (4, 6, 8, 10, 12) times, p1.

Work even until piece measures 2" (5 cm) from the beginning, ending with a WS row. Break yarn and transfer sts to st holder or waste yarn.

Back Hem

Work as for Front Hem until piece measures 2½" (6.5) cm, ending with a WS row. Do not break yarn. With RS of Back Hem facing, transfer Front Hem sts to same needle, so that they are to the left of Back Hem sts—188 (220, 252, 284, 316, 348) sts.

Join Hems

Change to larger circular needle.

Size Small Only

Set-Up Row (RS): *Knit to marker, increasing 2 sts evenly, sm, work Body Cable across 19 sts, work Wave Lace across 38 sts, work Body Cable across 19 sts, sm*, knit to end of Back Hem, increasing 2 sts evenly, pm; repeat from * to * for Front Hem, knit to end of Front Hem, increasing 2 sts evenly. Join for working in the rnd; pm for beginning of rnd—196 sts.

Size Medium Only

Set-Up Row (RS): *Knit to marker, sm, work Body Cable across 19 sts, work Wave Lace across 38 sts, work Body Cable across 19 sts, sm*, knit to end of Back Hem, pm; repeat from * to * for Front Hem, knit to end of Front Hem. Join for working in the rnd; pm for beginning of rnd—220 sts.

Sizes Large, X-Large, 2X-Large, and 3X-Large Only

Set-Up Row (RS): *Knit to marker, decreasing 0 (0, 2, 4, 6, 8) sts evenly, sm, work Body Cable across 19 sts, work Wave Lace across 38 sts, work Body Cable across 19 sts, sm*, knit to end of Back Hem, decreasing 0 (0, 2, 4, 6, 8) sts evenly, pm; repeat from * to * for Front Hem, knit to end of Front Hem, decreasing 0 (0, 2, 4, 6, 8) sts evenly. Join for working in the rnd; pm for beginning of rnd—0 (0, 244, 268, 292, 316) sts.

All Sizes

Working sts between markers in patterns as established and remaining sts in St st, work even until Back measures 16" (40.5 cm) from the beginning, ending with an even-numbered rnd of Wave Lace. Make note of last rnd of Body Cable worked. Do not break yarn.

SLEEVES

Using smaller needle(s) in your preferred style for knitting in the rnd, CO 56 (56, 56, 60, 64, 68) sts. Join for working in the rnd, being careful not to twist sts; pm for beginning of rnd.

Rnds 1-7: K1, *p2, k2; repeat from * to last st, k1.

Rnd 8: Work 28 (28, 28, 30, 32, 34) sts, M1R, work to end—57 (57, 57, 61, 65, 69) sts.

Rnd 9: K14 (14, 14, 16, 18, 20), pm, work Sleeve Cable across 29 sts, pm, knit to end.

Working sts between markers in pattern as established and remaining sts in St st, work even until piece measures 3½" (9 cm) from the beginning.

Shape Sleeve

Increase Rnd: K2, M1R, work to last 2 sts, M1L, k2—2 sts increased.

Repeat Increase Rnd every 14 (8, 6, 6, 4, 4) rnds 2 (4, 10, 14, 8, 14) times, then every 16 (10, 8, 8, 6, 6) rnds 4 (6, 4, 1, 10, 6) time(s)—71 (79, 87, 93, 103, 111) sts.

Work even until piece measures approximately 17" (43 cm) from the beginning, ending with same rnd of Sleeve Cable as for Body Cable. Break yarn and transfer first and last 6 (8, 10, 12, 14, 18) sts of rnd to st holder or waste yarn, removing marker—59 (63, 67, 69, 75, 75) sts remain.

YOKE

Joining Rnd: With RS of Body facing, using yarn attached to Front, and continuing in patterns as established, work 6 (8, 10, 12, 14, 18) sts and transfer last 12 (16, 20, 24, 28, 36) sts worked to st holder or waste yarn (removing marker), work across Back to 6 (8, 10, 12, 14, 18) sts before marker, pm, place next 12 (16, 20, 24, 28, 36) sts on st holder or waste yarn (removing marker), work across Left Sleeve, pm, work across Front, pm, work across Right Sleeve. Join for working in the rnd; pm for new beginning of rnd—290 (314, 338, 358, 386, 394) sts.

Work even for 1 rnd.

Shape Raglan and Back Neck

Note: *Body raglan shaping will be worked at different intervals than Sleeve raglan shaping. Instructions for both will be given separately, but will be worked at the same time. Back neck shaping will begin before raglan shaping has been completed. Please read entire section through before beginning.*

Body Raglan Decrease Rnd: [K1, ssk, work to 3 sts before next marker, k2tog, k1, sm, work to next marker, sm] twice—4 sts decreased.

Repeat Body Raglan Decrease Rnd every other rnd 4 (7, 8, 9, 10, 9) more times, every 4 rnds 8 (6, 6, 6, 6, 8) times, then every other rnd 4 (7, 8, 9, 10, 9) times. AT THE SAME TIME, beginning on first Body Raglan Decrease Rnd, shape Sleeves as follows:

Sleeve Raglan Decrease Rnd: [Work to marker, sm, k1, ssk, work to 3 sts before next marker, k2tog, k1, sm] twice—4 sts decreased.

Repeat Sleeve Raglan Decrease Rnd every other rnd 24 (26, 28, 14, 32, 15) more times, every 4 rnds 0 (0, 0, 1, 0, 2) time(s), then every other rnd 0 (0, 0, 14, 0, 15) times. AT THE SAME TIME, when 17 Sleeve sts remain, ending with a Decrease Rnd, shape Back neck as follows:

Note: *Neck is shaped using short rows.*

Next Rnd: Work to 3 sts before third marker (between Front and Right Sleeve).

Short Row 1 (RS): Continuing to work raglan decreases as established, work to fourth marker (between Left Sleeve and Front), work 16 (16, 17, 18, 19, 20) sts, w&t.

Short Row 2 (WS): Work to fourth marker (between Right Sleeve and Front), work 16 (16, 17, 18, 19, 20) sts, w&t.

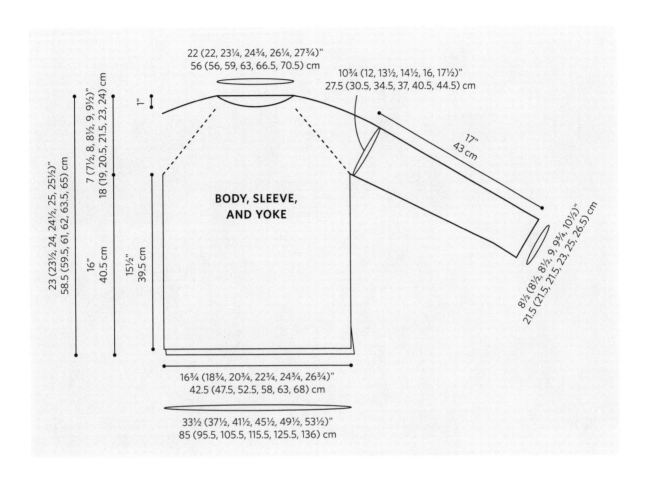

22 (22, 23¼, 24¾, 26¼, 27¾)"
56 (56, 59, 63, 66.5, 70.5) cm

10¾ (12, 13½, 14½, 16, 17½)"
27.5 (30.5, 34.5, 37, 40.5, 44.5) cm

1"

7 (7½, 8, 8½, 9, 9½)"
18 (19, 20.5, 21.5, 23, 24) cm

23 (23½, 24, 24½, 25, 25½)"
58.5 (59.5, 61, 62, 63.5, 65) cm

16"
40.5 cm

15½"
39.5 cm

17"
43 cm

8½ (8½, 8½, 9, 9¾, 10½)"
21.5 (21.5, 21.5, 23, 25, 26.5) cm

BODY, SLEEVE,
AND YOKE

16¾ (18¾, 20¾, 22¾, 24¾, 26¾)"
42.5 (47.5, 52.5, 58, 63, 68) cm

33½ (37½, 41½, 45½, 49½, 53½)"
85 (95.5, 105.5, 115.5, 125.5, 136) cm

Short Row 3: Work to 4 sts before wrapped st of previous RS row, w&t.

Short Row 4: Work to 4 sts before wrapped st of previous WS row, w&t.

Short Rows 5–8: Repeat Short Rows 3 and 4 twice—122 (122, 130, 138, 146, 154) sts remain when all raglan shaping is complete.

Short Row 9: Work to beginning-of-rnd marker (between Right Sleeve and Back), working wraps together with wrapped sts as you come to them.

Next Rnd: Change to smaller needle(s). Removing all markers except beginning-of-rnd marker and working wraps together with wrapped sts as you come to them, work in 2x2 Rib, decreasing 2 sts across Back as you work—120 (120, 128, 136, 144, 152) sts remain. Work even for 8 rnds.

BO all sts loosely in pattern.

FINISHING

Using Kitchener st, join underarm sts. Block piece as desired.

YARN /for/ THOUGHT

organic

Those who have been led by instinct to work with wool share similar experiences, whether they raise the sheep themselves or blend purchased fiber into the perfect yarn. Farming can be a call to carry on a family's heritage, maintain the land, create more open space, or interact more closely with nature. Fiber producers who learn to listen to their instincts are often better stewards of the flocks they tend, the machines they use, and the world in which they live. When you encounter someone passionate about their work, it shines through in everything they do, and yarn is no exception.

Each of the fiber producers in this section is familiar with materials that might seem unusual to others. Whether they aim to gather what is already there, revive the forgotten, or conserve a way of life, they work within the life cycle of what is around them and adapt it to create special, unique materials.

A VERB FOR KEEPING WARM

Deeply entrenched in the history of textile dyeing and production, California-based Kristine Vejar's vast experience and research results in a line of carefully sourced yarns that she then dyes using a spectacular palette of organic elements. Pioneer, a yarn made of California-raised, processed, and dyed 100 percent Merino wool, is one part of the ambitious California Wool Project. The goal of the project is to revitalize the wool textile industry in the state by supporting farmers and US mills, creating beautiful yarns in the process.

CESTARI SHEEP & WOOL

Francis Chester and his signature cream-colored cowboy hat can be easily spotted in the Cestari fiber booth at any festival. This Virginia-based farmer and rancher has a passion for making wool that extends far beyond his own flock. When local farmers were losing their farms to foreclosures and the textile mills were closing due to better pricing overseas, Chester went to work, buying a mill and relocating it to Virginia so he could source, prepare, process, and dye yarns domestically on American soil. The mill uses a variety of processes designed to clean and prep the wools without damaging them, maintaining the natural character and voice of the material. This family business supports many farmers and ranchers across the country.

BUFFALO GOLD

The decline of the American Bison is one of the saddest chapters of American history. Hunted and driven from their vast prairie range by settlers seeking better lives out West, the bison was driven to near extinction and is only around today due to the careful conservation efforts of people like the Miskins, who own and operate Buffalo Gold. Bison produce a dark, silky soft fiber that knits up beautifully into amazingly warm garments and accessories, perfect for winter warming.

experiment
fearlessly

IN THE PROCESS OF DEVELOPING an understanding and love for knitting and fiber, it is easy to fall into comfort patterns with our skills and materials. But when we explore new techniques and supplies and give ourselves time to learn and embrace them rather than just making assumptions about them, we open up a whole new world of possibilities as makers.

My fiber comfort zone has always been round, energetic wools. I have found through my experimentation with spinning various wool breeds that I value certain fiber characteristics above others; I prefer them not too soft and not too coarse. For me, a bit of springiness is just right. It sometimes takes a lot of effort for me to move beyond what I love to a slinky, silky yarn, even if it is a wonderful example of the fiber and the pattern is begging for it. I have never thought of myself as someone particularly fond of alpaca, for example; I find it weighty and itchy. But when I took the time to learn more about the fiber, I discovered that there are two main types: Huacaya alpaca is fluffy and cloud-like, while Suri alpaca has longer, shinier fibers that create luxurious garments with incredible drape, perfect for a wrap or a scarf in fluid, delicate lace.

A diet comprised of even our favorite foods can lose our interest after a short time. The same goes for making—when knitters spend too much time growing accustomed to the same material, we lose the fervor of discovery that came to us when first learning. Like a cardinal in fresh snow, something new and bright can be the surprising jolt we need to regain wonder and excitement.

Slow knitting is not just about pushing ourselves out of our comfort zones, but reevaluating those zones and asking ourselves why we have them. Often, these issues stem from our own soft spots: The knitter who hates double-pointed needles because she never learned to balance them during cast-on. The knitter who dislikes charts because he was confused and overwhelmed by the first ones he tried. When we step beyond what scares us to give new techniques and patterns a chance, we open ourselves to opportunity.

Confidence in knitting doesn't come from knowing everything. To the contrary, exploration is key to being comfortable with taking on patterns that might challenge you. Finding a project you are passionate about making, or a yarn you are excited to use, can be a great initial first step to reaching beyond your current skill set. The motivation behind starting the project should be to create something beautiful and learn along the way.

Another great way to step out of your comfort zone is to explore new stitches. New knitters can extend their basic knit and purl knowledge by pursuing patterns that use these stitches in fresh or complex ways. Incorporating texture into larger, varied pieces (like those found in a sweater) can help you understand how they form.

For cables, an often anxiety-inducing skill for new knitters, a bit-by-bit approach may help complex twists seem more accessible. Divide the chart into logical start and finish points, marking each section off on the left side with a highlighter based on how much time you can dedicate to the project each time you sit down. I find that cables pair nicely with a bit of background music or an audio book, in hour-long stretches. Adding a lifeline—running a bit of dental floss or contrast-colored thread through the final row in each section—can feel like an accomplishment and aid in fixing any errors later.

Reward yourself between difficult sections by working on a bit of mindless Stockinette in a simpler project. Lace panels can be worked in the same way, even those with wrong-side stitch manipulation. Print out separate pages for the charts and written instructions, and never be afraid to make notes in the margins. Patterns you purchase are yours: Do not be afraid to mark them up and take ownership of them. Above all, dive in fearlessly and learn as you go! We become better makers through practice and the admission (and repair) of errors. Each mistake is an opportunity to learn and better understand the underlying structure of how knitting works.

As much as we fall into patterns with the fibers and the techniques we use, we often have unexpected biases toward different methods, too. It is easy to get caught up in your own preferences of what *should* be done and attempt to sway or force others to your way of thinking. One of my biggest biases has to do with the care of my handmade items. I hold a strong personal belief that there is intrinsic value in the fact that the things I make by hand are delicate and special and should be taken care of in a detailed way. I don't mind handwashing or line drying; I rather enjoy the process. I have been known to carefully tend to a basin of handknit socks, delicately pushing the water out of them as they dry and hanging each one gingerly by a single clothespin. I have meticulously ironed handmade quilts so they have just the right amount of crispness. I am the crafter who sits each weekend and de-pills my cashmere and steams my mohair sweaters to get *just the right bloom.* I find enjoyment in the upkeep and can be easily put off by the words "just throw it in the wash." It is the knitter like myself, who shares these views toward the meticulous care of handmade things, who often scorns superwash wools (wools that have been treated to be machine washable) for many reasons—because they are not traditionally eco-friendly, because they remove something essentially "wooly" about the fiber, or because they leave the yarn with less elasticity and a "squeaky" finish.

When I released myself from these restrictions, I was pleased to discover that more difficult caring methods and exacting fibers are not necessarily better, just different. Fiber manufacturing has come a long way, and now there are several environmentally conscious superwash wools being produced by people who care just as much about the fiber and its character as I do. Even better, they're able to embrace the other elements that make superwash appealing—superwashed wool takes color brilliantly, in every shade and hue. Because of the smooth nature of these yarns, they are also a bit shiny, making hanks of them the purest form of wooly eye-candy. Knitting with bright, colorful yarn is fun, especially when you can gift the finished piece without worrying about how it will be treated.

Take the time to evaluate things you avoid in your knitting, and really think about why. Knitting is a craft, learned over time and honed with practice. By challenging ourselves to embrace something new, we become more creative and have more opportunity to make projects we love. It is all well and good to talk about the merits of one fiber, technique, or method over another, but by giving ourselves restrictions, we are excluding so many things we may have otherwise enjoyed. This is unnecessary! Fiber is extremely versatile, and it is easy to find a bridge rather than force a leap across the gap with a little digging into the why and how of things. Cultivate your knowledge of the things you use, keep your standards high, take time to research, explore, and expand, and be fearless in your pursuit of making.

next steps

Innovation often comes out of accepting a challenge rather than avoiding it. Slow knitting allows us the time to delve into the unknown and unfamiliar and encourages us to spend the time needed to work our way through problems that may arise. Our knitter's conscience will tell us when we should step away from a project, when a yarn and pattern are not in agreement, or even when we're about to run out before getting to that bind-off row. The passion we have for the project, the materials, and the process will drive us to try again when we are ready.

While it might seem like a daunting task, it is possible to take small steps toward new knitting experiences without feeling as if you are diving headfirst into frustration. If you find yourself relying heavily on knits and purls, attempt to learn how to manipulate a few stitches for a subtly textured stitch pattern before graduating to cables. Adding a break of yarnovers and knit-two-togethers into straight Stockinette can help prepare you for the increases and decreases that come with more difficult lace motifs.

Similarly, if you find large-scale projects worrying, increase size slowly from smaller pieces you're comfortable with, learning what you'll need for garments as you go. While an unassuming set of mittens teaches the construction of a cuff, the increase of a sleeve might be hidden in the development of a thumb gusset. A cowl or scarf is great practice for expanses of Stockinette—working through these stitches in a repetitive way teaches your fingers how to feel when a stitch is facing the wrong way or is doubled up.

You can also challenge yourself by trying new materials. If you find yourself primarily using animal fibers, branch out into the world of plants and even synthetics: bamboo, cotton, corn, and fibers spun from milk casein provide new experiences. While you may find the absence of wool simply makes your love of it grow fonder, you will know what wool might do when blended with one of these unusual materials and prepare yourself for the use of them.

All too often we place restrictions on ourselves about what colors or materials we can and cannot wear, but knitters who try new things also learn to allow themselves to express who they are freely. Making clothing by hand is indulgent: It's all about taking time for yourself, learning new skills, and wearing the results proudly. By allowing ourselves this luxury, we knit more vividly and live more fully, embracing and discovering who we are in each stitch along the way.

Through knitting, we transform the yarn into our own artworks, expressing who we are as knitters in our choice of patterns, stitches, and garments. One person might prioritize a yarn's stitch definition, while another celebrates color through playful pattern. Perhaps that's the most beautiful part of all: Each finished piece is a collaboration between you and the producer, expanding on their original vision with your own imagination. By fearlessly diving into the world of expressive, living color, we give ourselves leave to form emotional attachment to our knitting and the process of making.

What you make may not always work out as expected, or you may not like the finished product, but you will have learned something in the making of it. In life we learn from our mistakes, and in knitting we can do the same, turning them instead into experiences that can inform us and encourage us to reach for the new, different, and exciting.

o-wool

The relationships yarn companies form with their customers in the first few years are usually dependent on specific yarns. Customers become familiar and comfortable with existing yarns and reach for them time and time again. Such was the case with O-Wool, a line of yarns produced by the Vermont Organic Fiber Company. Produced using organic Merino wool before it became more commonplace and available, these milled yarns became favorites of a loyal market that was baffled when the company decided to liquidate this line, selling it off to Jocelyn Tunney in 2010.

Jocelyn Tunney was familiar with the yarn industry through her work with Fairmount Fibers, a distributor of fine handknitting yarns in North America, long before she bought the O-Wool yarn line. Inspired by her work with Uruguayan yarn brand Manos del Uruguay and armed with the knowledge she'd gained repping yarns and working in yarn stores, Jocelyn felt ready to tackle the challenge of owning and distributing her own brand. For a designer passionate about eco-conscious product and great wools, the O-Wool brand seemed like an ideal jumping-off point, with an existing customer base that loved and knew the product.

While the loyal customer base who knew the O-Wool line loved the rustic, dense yarns spun by the original mill, the burgeoning market of newly formed knitters (fresh off the knitting rush of 2005 and 2006) were used to ultra-soft Merinos and silky synthetics. Jocelyn knew that new branding wouldn't be the only change she needed to make to reach the market in a larger way. She bravely set about redefining the company's existing lines—Balance, Legacy, and Classic—to fit more with the modern knitting market's needs. Jocelyn had two main goals in mind: affordability for the average knitter, and yarns that could continue to be classics in a plethora of colorways.

Jocelyn made great use of her skills in marketing and design, releasing pattern after pattern in beautiful, attainable shapes that kept knitters following the company for staple accessory pieces. The simple, fresh branding was working. New versions of the yarns were sold only online direct-to-consumer to keep costs accessible to knitters of all budgets, a practice unheard of in an industry largely dependent on physical handling for sales. Jocelyn began making moves to do something else unexpected for eco-conscious brands: She developed O-Wash, a superwash line.

At the time, "superwash" seemed to be synonymous with chemicals, greenhouse gas emissions, and water waste. Traditional superwash treatments are far from organic or environmentally friendly, and many are conducted in countries all over the world that have lax emissions standards that allow them to damage water sources and create runoff that affects plant, marine, and human living conditions in the areas where they are used.

Jocelyn did not want to damage the brand that she had rebuilt, but superwash wools had become a staple in the handknitting market.

Many knitters, dedicated to making things for family members or young children, scoffed (and still do) at the idea of using anything other than a washable yarn for gifts and garments. O-Wool, Jocelyn felt, needed a washable option, but it also needed to embody the environmental sensibilities that had made O-Wool unique in the first place. Thus began the period of research and development leading up to the release of O-Wash.

O-Wash is treated using an organic polymer that glazes the individual wool fibers, preventing the wool's scales from interlocking, or felting, during washing. For anyone who has worked with a traditionally superwashed wool, you may be familiar with a slight "squeakiness" from the smoother fibers. While O-Wash is certainly smoother and less "grabby" than an untreated Merino, it lacks this squeaky quality, and it has a matte finish (like standard Merino wool) rather than the sheen attributed to most washable wools. Upon handling, you can still feel the character of the wool—what makes this yarn recognizably Merino has not been lost.

Additionally, O-Wash makes use of one of the most attractive qualities of superwash wools (in addition to washability, of course). Superwashed Merino takes color brilliantly, as evidenced in the constantly growing color card accompanying O-Wash weights. The palette is a jewel-box of coral, gold, and garnet, with a large range of blues and neutrals ideal for almost any application.

O-Wash—and the modern-day iteration of O-Wool—has certainly reached the goals that Jocelyn Tunney set out to achieve. By thinking outside her own fiber comfort zone and pushing beyond what was typically "acceptable" content for an environmentally conscientious wool, Jocelyn updated this popular workhorse yarn line for the modern era, maintaining the principles of sustainability and celebration of natural wools O-Wool was founded on while embracing the needs of the average knitter.

Myrtus

Designed by Kirsten Kapur

O-Wash fingering's 2-ply structure makes it a bit delicate for socks but perfect for fingering-weight lace motifs. Next-to-skin soft, this luxurious paneled lace wrap is perfect for light layering about your shoulders or wrapping several times about the neck on the chilliest of days. Superwash yarn lends durability to otherwise delicate lace, taking the fear out of aggressive blocking for those experimenting with lace knitting.

FINISHED MEASUREMENTS

Approximately 20" (51 cm) wide x 74" (188 cm) long, after blocking

YARN

O-Wool O-Wash Fingering [100% machine-washable certified organic Merino wool; 428 yards (391 meters)/ 3½ ounces (100 grams)]: 3 hanks Devil's Pool

NEEDLES

One pair straight needles size US 5 (3.75 mm)

Change needle size if necessary to obtain correct gauge.

NOTIONS

Stitch markers

GAUGE

18 sts and 33½ rows = 4" (10 cm) in Lace Pattern, after blocking

STITCH PATTERNS

FULL EYELET PATTERN

(odd number of sts; 4-row repeat)
Row 1 (RS): K2, *yo, k2tog; repeat from * to last st, k1.
Row 2: K2, purl to last 2 sts, k2.
Row 3: K1, *ssk, yo; repeat from * to last 2 sts, k2.
Row 4: Repeat Row 2.
Repeat Rows 1–4 for Full Eyelet Pattern.

RIGHT EYELET PATTERN

(odd number of sts; 4-row repeat)
Row 1 (RS): K2, *yo, k2tog; repeat from * to last st, k1.
Row 2: Purl to last 2 sts, k2.
Row 3: K1, *ssk, yo; repeat from * to end.
Row 4: Repeat Row 2.
Repeat Rows 1–4 for Right Eyelet Pattern.

LEFT EYELET PATTERN

(odd number of sts; 4-row repeat)
Row 1 (RS): *Yo, k2tog; repeat from * to last st, k1.
Row 2: K2, purl to end.
Row 3: K1, *ssk, yo; repeat from * to last 2 sts, k2.
Row 4: Repeat Row 2.
Repeat Rows 1–4 for Left Eyelet Pattern.

LACE PATTERN (see Chart)

(multiple of 24 sts + 5; 48-row repeat)
Note: If using markers between repeats, it will be necessary to remove the markers to complete the decreases on Rows 7, 15, 23, 33, 39, and 45; replace the markers before the completed decreases.
Row 1 (RS): K2, *k4, [yo, ssk] twice, k1, k2tog, yo, k3, yo, ssk, k1, [k2tog, yo] twice, k3; repeat from * to last 3 sts, k3.
Row 2 and all WS Rows: Purl.
Row 3: K2, *k2, k2tog, yo, k1, yo, ssk, yo, sk2p, yo, k5, yo, k3tog, yo, k2tog, yo, k1, yo, ssk, k1; repeat from * to last 3 sts, k3.
Row 5: K2, *k1, k2tog, yo, k3, [yo, ssk] twice, k5, [k2tog, yo] twice, k3, yo, ssk; repeat from * to last 3 sts, k3.
Row 7: K1, yo, *sk2p, yo, k5, yo, ssk, k1, ssk, yo, k1, yo, k2tog, k1, k2tog, yo, k5, yo; repeat from * to last 4 sts, sk2p, yo, k1.
Row 9: K2, *k2, yo, ssk, k4, yo, ssk, k1, yo, s2kp2, yo, k1, k2tog, yo, k4, k2tog, yo, k1; repeat from * to last 3 sts, k3.
Row 11: K2, *k3, yo, ssk, k4, yo, sk2p, yo, k1, yo, k3tog, yo, k4, k2tog, yo, k2; repeat from * to last 3 sts, k3.
Row 13: K2tog, yo, *[k1, yo, ssk] twice, k4, yo, ssk, k1, k2tog, yo, k4, k2tog, yo, k1, k2tog, yo; repeat from * to last 3 sts, k1, yo, ssk.

Row 15: K1, yo, *s2kp2, yo, k2, k2tog, yo, k5, yo, sk2p, yo, k5, yo, ssk, k2, yo; repeat from * to last 4 sts, s2kp2, yo, k1.

Row 17: Ssk, yo, *k1, yo, [k2tog] twice, yo, k4, k2tog, yo, k3, yo, ssk, k4, yo, [ssk] twice, yo; repeat from * to last 3 sts, k1, yo, k2tog.

Row 19: K2, *k2, k2tog, yo, k4, [k2tog, yo] twice, k1, [yo, ssk] twice, k4, yo, ssk, k1; repeat from * to last 3 sts, k3.

Row 21: K2, *k1, k2tog, yo, k4, k2tog, yo, k2, yo, s2kp2, yo, k2, yo, ssk, k4, yo, ssk; repeat from * to last 3 sts, k3.

Row 23: K1, yo, *sk2p, yo, k4, k2tog, yo, k2, ssk, yo, k1, yo, k2tog, k2, yo, ssk, k4, yo; repeat from * to last 4 sts, sk2p, yo, k1.

Row 25: K2, *k2, yo, ssk, k1, [k2tog, yo] twice, k7, [yo, ssk] twice, k1, k2tog, yo, k1; repeat from * to last 3 sts, k3.

Row 27: K2, *k3, yo, k3tog, yo, k2tog, yo, k1, yo, ssk, k3, k2tog, yo, k1, yo, ssk, yo, sk2p, yo, k2; repeat from * to last 3 sts, k3.

Row 29: K2, *k3, [k2tog, yo] twice, k3, yo, ssk, k1, k2tog, yo, k3, [yo, ssk] twice, k2; repeat from * to last 3 sts, k3.

Row 31: Ssk, yo, *k1, yo, k2tog, k1, k2tog, yo, k5, yo, sk2p, yo, k5, yo, ssk, k1, ssk, yo; repeat from * to last 3 sts, k1, yo, k2tog.

Row 33: K1, yo, *s2kp2, yo, k1, k2tog, yo, k4, k2tog, yo, k3, yo, ssk, k4, yo, ssk, k1, yo; repeat from * to last 4 sts, s2kp2, yo, k1.

Row 35: Ssk, yo, *k1, yo, k3tog, yo, k4, k2tog, yo, k5, yo, ssk, k4, yo, sk2p, yo; repeat from * to last 3 sts, k1, yo, k2tog.

Row 37: K2, *k1, k2tog, yo, k4, [k2tog, yo, k1] twice, yo, ssk, k1, yo, ssk, k4, yo, ssk; repeat from * to last 3 sts, k3.

Row 39: K1, yo, *sk2p, yo, k5, yo, ssk, k2, yo, s2kp2, yo, k2, k2tog, yo, k5, yo; repeat from * to last 3 sts, sk2p, yo, k1.

Row 41: K2, *k2, yo, ssk, k4, yo, [ssk] twice, yo, k1, yo, [k2tog] twice, yo, k4, k2tog, yo, k1; repeat from * to last 3 sts, k3.

Row 43: K2tog, yo, *k1, [yo, ssk] twice, k4, yo, ssk, k3, k2tog, yo, k4, [k2tog, yo] twice; repeat from * to last 3 sts, k1, yo, ssk.

Row 45: K1, yo, *s2kp2, yo, k2, yo, ssk, k4, yo, ssk, k1, k2tog, yo, k4, k2tog, yo, k2, yo; repeat from * to last 4 sts, s2kp2, yo, k1.

Row 47: Ssk, yo, *k1, yo, k2tog, k2, yo, ssk, k4, yo, sk2p, yo, k4, k2tog, yo, k2, ssk, yo; repeat from * to last 3 sts, k1, yo, k2tog.

Row 48: Purl.
Repeat Rows 1–48 for Lace Pattern.

PATTERN NOTE
You may work Lace Pattern from the text or chart.

LACE PATTERN

Chart legend:

Symbol	Meaning
☐	Knit on RS, purl on WS.
O	Yo
⟋	K2tog
⟍	Ssk
⟋	K3tog
⟑	Sk2p
⊥	S2kp2

24-st panel

48-row repeat

WRAP

Border

CO 87 sts.

Knit 2 rows.

Work Rows 1–4 of Full Eyelet Pattern 10 times.

Body

Set-Up Row (RS): Work Right Eyelet Pattern over 17 sts, pm, work Lace Pattern to last 17 sts, pm, work Left Eyelet Pattern to end.

Continuing to work Lace Pattern between markers and Right and Left Eyelet Patterns outside markers as established, work Rows 2–48 of Lace Pattern once, Rows 1–48 nine times, then Rows 1–28 once, removing markers on final row.

Border

Work Rows 1–4 of Full Eyelet Pattern 10 times.

Knit 2 rows.

BO Row (RS): *K2tog-tbl, slip st back to left-hand needle; repeat from * until all sts have been BO.

Finishing

Block to measurements.

jill draper makes stuff

A few years ago, there was a buzz online about a new dyer who was releasing US-sourced, spun, and dyed wools. They came in standard hanks, but one of the bases, a sweater-weight wool, was offered in a jumbo skein. Knitters visiting fiber festivals throughout the upper East Coast would post pictures of themselves holding up skeins as big as their heads, watermelon-size trophy balls of yarn that could knit up whole sweaters in a single bound (with only two ends to weave in). These monster skeins were dyed in a range of colors that would be the envy of any paint box—emerald greens and mustard yellows, maraschino cherry red, and soft, gentle pinks. The base is called Empire, and it's dyed by Jill Draper. Her company is called Jill Draper Makes Stuff, a name that perfectly describes what she does.

Jill grew up with a passion for art that eventually translated into a degree in fashion design, inspired by fashion icons Vivienne Westwood and Zandra Rhodes. To her, fashion was wearable artwork, used like a second skin to communicate her personality to the world. Her unique blend of punk, grunge, and vivid color set her apart from other students during her time studying at the Pratt Institute, where she used the "old way" of knitting to create unique new textures for her final collection. Models adorned with handknit tops stalked the runway in her senior show. After graduation, Jill worked with fashion companies and mills, developing textiles and garments using fibers sourced all over the world, but continued to research knitting and harbor a love for the handcraft she had explored in college.

Inspired by the story of Morehouse Farm's yarns, entirely made in the USA, and Melanie Falick's *Knitting in America*, Jill decided to move to the Hudson Valley to pursue a dream of making fibers from scratch collaboratively with the mills in the Northeast. New England was one of the few areas of the country uniquely poised to deliver the range of materials and methods that she had carefully researched, and she took up a job where she could learn how the yarns were made.

Over time, she decided to make her own yarns, based on the skills she had acquired and her natural love of textiles and material manipulation. Jill developed a manifesto for her yarn line—yarns should be sheep to skein, never sourced or sent offshore, and should be conscientious of materials and resources. An avid color lover (there's only one black dress in her closet), Jill began dyeing yarns in a wild array of colors. Her bases also feature yarns named for the places they come from: Mohonk, Esopus, Empire, Rifton. Knitters snatch them up at fiber festivals or at the few yarn stores that are lucky enough to carry her lines.

Each year, Jill seems to release new, tantalizing visual textures for us to explore: marled yarns with one dark and one light ply, dyed in rich jewel tones; a swirl of gradient, soft-spun wooly singles wound into bull's-eye cakes and stacked like Wisconsin Cheddar; a chunky, haloed blend of mohair and Corriedale wool that seems to

float like tiny clouds into hands and baskets. She is endlessly experimenting and trying new textures, dye methods, and fibers.

I first encountered Jill's yarns for myself at Vogue Knitting Live in New York in early 2015. Her booth opens each show packed to the gills with color and slowly empties out throughout the event, sometimes with only a single dye lot in a sought-after colorway. Those who know her brand eagerly make way to the vast array, hand-picking which treasures will come home with them and jealously hoarding skeins in the decision making process, arms laden and overflowing before they release and sort their piles on round, cloth-adorned tables. I remember looking through the racks twice only to find that one of the colors I had been considering had already been snatched up, and I saw it in the work of a well-known knitting designer a few months later.

While each base is special and unique (Empire, after all, has a cult following), I immediately fell for Hudson, a superwash yarn that falls somewhere between DK and worsted. Named for where the wool is sourced (in the Hudson River Valley of New York) and superwashed here in the USA, Hudson is made using a process that reuses water and has a low impact on the environment. I love Hudson's springy, energetic nature. Overspun in the very best of ways, this yarn is round and fun to knit with, and is almost eager to become something highly textured, cabled, and colorful. I have personally knit several projects in this yarn and can never seem to get enough, despite my methods of resistance.

Buying enough yarn is crucial with Jill's yarns, as they're unlikely to show up in the same place in the same shades twice. This presents a unique challenge for knitters who are used to the "try it and buy it" method of yarn purchasing. Competing with the masses for a color at a major fiber show means that buyers must dive in headfirst to the idea of a project in an eye-catching hue, acting on their initial gut reaction rather than careful planning and purchasing. This type of emotional purchase is one I usually discourage, but Jill's yarns give me an opportunity to break tradition and reward my inner painter. I have a bad habit of collecting her skeins whenever I see them. A sweater lot in deep sapphire blue. A single skein in the sweetest peachy-pink. A yellow green the exact color of peony buds. They excite and inspire me when I see them sitting and waiting to become—they beckon me to cast on and experiment.

Most of all, they return me to the place that I first found them. Jill's colors are textile memories you can take home and knit with whenever you need a little revival. They communicate so much more than a simple violet, yellow, or red. Her skeins are moments in time and feelings that we love to have: an array of changing, golden leaves in thin, crisp autumn. The rippling, pale blue-greens of the ocean against white sand beaches. The bright, shining radiance of a single, perfect clementine. For those feelings encapsulated in fiber form, I will take the risk of collecting a bit too much yarn, on occasion.

Spruce

Designed by Meghan Fernandes

Designer Meghan Fernandes takes advantage of the bouncy, squishy structure of Jill Draper's Hudson yarn by using it to create cables and brioche—two textures that require extra care and time to master. Simple but sophisticated, this cowl is a piece that can be worn season after season. The adventurous knitter will enjoy the thought that goes into working brioche in the round, as well as the satisfaction of creating double-sided cables. Wear the cowl folded double and pulled down slightly over the tops of the shoulders for snuggly warmth.

FINISHED MEASUREMENTS
31" (78.5 cm) circumference x 12" (30.5 cm) tall

YARN
Jill Draper Makes Stuff Hudson [100% superwash Merino wool; 240 yards (219 meters) / 3.74 ounces (106 grams)]: 2 skeins Spruce

NEEDLE
Size US 8 (5 mm) circular needle 24–32" (60–80 cm) long

Change needle size if necessary to obtain correct gauge.

NOTIONS
Stitch marker; cable needle

GAUGE
17 sts and 24 counted rnds (48 worked rnds) = 4" (10 cm) in Brioche Rib
Note: See Pattern Notes for information on counting sts and rnds.

SPECIAL ABBREVIATIONS
BrC12F: Slip 6 sts to cable needle and hold to front, [brk, sl1yo] 3 times, [brk, sl1yo] 3 times from cable needle.
Brk (brioche knit, also known as bark): Knit the st (that was slipped in the rnd before) together with its yo.
Brp (brioche purl, also known as burp): Purl the st (that was slipped in the rnd before) together with its yo.
Sl1yo: With yarn in front, slip 1 st purlwise, then bring yarn over needle (and over slipped st) to back of work.

STITCH PATTERN
BRIOCHE STITCH RIB
(even number of sts; 2-rnd repeat)
Rnd 1: Sl1yo, brp; repeat from * to end.
Rnd 2: *Brk, sl1yo; repeat from * to end.
Repeat Rnds 1 and 2 for Brioche Stitch Rib.

PATTERN NOTES
When counting stitches, always count the stitch and its following yarnover as one stitch; never count the yarnover as a stitch. When counting rounds, for each stitch visible in the knit column, count two rounds.

COWL

Using Long-Tail CO (see Special Techniques, page 167), loosely CO 150 sts. Join for working in the rnd, being careful not to twist sts; pm for beginning of rnd.

Set-Up Rnd: *K1, sl1yo; repeat from * to end.
Work Rnds 1 and 2 of Brioche Stitch Rib 4 times, then work Rnd 1 once more.

Cable Rnd: [Brk, sl1yo] 6 times, brC12F, [brk, sl1yo] 31 times, brC12F, [brk, sl1yo] 26 times.

*Work Rnds 1 and 2 of Brioche Stitch Rib 20 times, then work Rnd 1 once more.
Work Cable Rnd once.
Repeat from * 2 more times.

Work Rnds 1 and 2 of Brioche Stitch Rib 4 times.

BO all sts loosely in pattern.

YARN /for/ THOUGHT

innovation

Forgotten or simply fallen out of favor, a new-to-you material may be just what your knitting needs. The producers below offer some of my favorite alternatives to the embrace of familiar wools. While fiber is the product of careful, centuries-long livestock cultivation, sometimes it becomes necessary for someone to come along and remind knitters of why it was well-loved in the first place.

FANCY TIGER CRAFTS

This yarn and fabric store based in Denver, Colorado, has far exceeded the expectations of owner-operators Jamie Jennings and Amber Corcoran, and is now a beacon of inspiration for garment makers worldwide. Fancy Tiger's line of in-house yarns is worthy of the brand's reputation. I particularly love two of these wools for garments, but for entirely different reasons. Heirloom, a celebratory 100 percent US-grown-and-milled Romney longwool in a riot of heathered colors, is ideal for outer-layers with a bit of sheen. Junegrass, a limited edition Colorado-sourced-and-spun wool featuring a Rambouillet and Merino cross, is ideal for next-to-skin wear. By highlighting these different qualities in the same medium (wool), Fancy Tiger encourages knitters everywhere to reevaluate and explore what they think they know about one of the world's favorite fibers.

SALT RIVER MILLS

I hesitate to say that anyone in the yarn industry is reinventing the wheel, but in many ways, the North American Suri Company is doing just that under its Salt River Mills label. There are two types of alpaca: Suri and Huacaya. Huacaya is the type most knitters are familiar with. Suri is less common, especially in the handknitting market, partially due to the animal's attractiveness. When a small team of entrepreneurial Suri alpaca lovers formed a committee designed to increase the visibility of Suri as a potential fiber source in the United States, Liz Vahlkamp found herself learning how to gather, grade, spin, and sell Suri alpaca fiber to a market that had long forgotten its existence. Now she buys fleeces from more than forty farms in the US and Canada and is working to revive this luxury fiber's presence in yarn stores and fashion lines. She has even helped develop breeding plans that make the fleeces more marketable on a larger scale.

ANGORAGARNET

One of the hardest fibers to source ethically is angora. Unless you have been lucky enough to find a small-scale angora producer that clips or hand combs the fur, chances are that a high-quality, animal-cruelty-free version of this fiber has avoided your grasp. The revival of interest in Bohus-style colorwork and the subsequent release of knitting patterns from the Bohus Stickning fashion line (based in Bohuslän, a Northern Swedish province) has helped bring angora-blended yarns back into the public eye. AngoraGarnet, a Bohuslän-based angora fiber business, is dedicated to the ethical and careful raising of Angora rabbits, whose fur is then blended with Merino into yarns similar to those used at Bohus Stickning and dyed in a fabulous range of colorwork-worthy tones. This family-owned operation is dedicated to sharing the history of Bohus Stickning with the world, and it releases kits in collaboration with former Bohus designers and others who've created their own Bohus-inspired designs.

CHAPTER 5

explore openly

OVER THE PAST DECADE, KNITTING has transitioned into a new era. New Internet offerings and the rise of sites devoted to current knitting patterns and sharing inspiration with others have made knitting a truly global experience; knitters who live on opposite sides of the world can freely and openly explore other knitters' cultures and projects. Online forums are full of knitters asking for advice, sharing creative thoughts, and exploring their passion for fiber individually and as part of a greater whole. New pattern sources have become available to crafters in this way as well—magazines with smaller, limited print runs, or digital publications produced on small budgets by single designers create a feeling of closeness with those who supply inspiration and materials. Pattern designers have risen to celebrity status, with thousands of followers who await their latest release eagerly, needles in hand. Books are abundant, full of ideas for what to make and wear, with publishers quick to jump on the latest trends and revive interest in techniques and fibers from generations past.

Occasionally, I ponder what people before the Internet must have experienced when traveling to new places. At the age of fifteen, my great-great-grandmother was married and moved to Montana with her new husband to become a sod-house homesteader. Traveling by train and wagon across the country, she must have felt such isolation and fear, leaving family and friends to pursue a better life somewhere she had never been. I imagine that she had not only these anxieties, but also a residing sense of wonder, excitement, and anticipation of what their new home might bring. I know little of her journey, true thoughts, or experiences, but I do know that she was a crocheter, and she spent many nights in the sod house edging the household linens and making an endless supply of doilies. She drew comfort from what she knew and applied it to what she did not. When they moved back East, she brought these handmade pieces with her, where they would help her remember her time out West. It is interesting to me that these items can transition from being anchors to the present to memories of our past.

This global scope of knitting has extended to fiber availability as well. Walk into a yarn store and you're sure to discover not only a variety of wool—Merino, Corriedale, and Bluefaced Leicester (BFL) are some of the most common—but also a wide variety of exotic fibers. Alpaca, cashmere, mohair, silk, cotton, and bamboo have all become part of the standard knitter's repertoire. Go to a fiber show and you may encounter Angora, yak, possum, or bison hiding among the booths and stands. Our world of fiber is only restricted by what can be imported and cultivated. Producers mark where the fiber comes from and what variety it is: Mulberry silk, Muga silk; organic, natural-colored, Cleaner Cotton™; Suri alpaca, Huacaya alpaca. As crafters, we are spoiled for choice; long gone are the days of knitting only with yarns available at your local shops.

This abundance of information and products has made it possible for knitters to explore different countries, cultures, and knitting practices from the comfort of home. Noro, a popular yarn brand known for interesting color application, embraces the Japanese art of repair and appreciation of the imperfect known as *wabi-sabi*. In complex patterning, the beauty of Noro's yarn is lost, but knit a humble swatch of garter stitch and the thick and thin bumps and color changes can be celebrated. Icelandic Lopi, partially unspun and delicate, gains new strength when knit at the tight recommended gauge; designed to keep out wind and last through many winters, this rough wool makes for a cohesive knit fabric, resulting in cozy sweaters that wear like iron against the elements. Shetland wool sheep have been bred to have a dual coat—the soft, lightweight undercoat produces yarns that show off the delicate detail of fine lace, while the bouncy, heavier outer coat is suitable for winter-worthy thicker layers. Even unique cultural thoughts and practices can be translated through fiber. Hygge, a bulky, thick, and slightly brushed wool from Woolfolk, explores the Danish concept of the same name, embracing and facilitating a warm and welcoming atmosphere.

Other yarns may have more of a direct connection to the place from which they come. Many wools being made available are only possible through the conservation efforts of countries or small farms. Often, a brand has a single individual running the entire business, from raising the sheep and milling the yarns to dyeing by hand.

Researching a yarn and the history of its making allows you to travel the world from the comfort of your own home. Understanding the tradition and culture surrounding the materials you use infuses your project with another layer of dimensionality that will add to the passion and excitement of casting on. The time involved with exploring and discovering the details about the materials we use is just as sacred as the time spent transforming them into garments we will cherish.

next steps

The Internet age has given us many advantages when it comes to travel. We are able to access abundant stores of accurate information about the places we are headed, allowing us to plan our adventure accordingly. A knitting project is often like a well-planned trip: We know all of the required pieces and where they fit. If we have been practicing slow knitting, we may have done the research needed beforehand to make sure that where we are headed is exactly where we want to go. Our experiences have informed us, and we have a bank of knowledge to draw on from others who have taken the path before us.

We can explore our knitting more openly by exploring our yarn and fiber more intimately. While we might come to each project armed with the knowledge and materials to create it, we should also come to each new cast-on with a sense of the unknown. Take the time to revel in the anticipation of starting fresh with new materials. Prepare yourself to learn something from the tactile, physical experience, and not just from words you've read. Create an adventure out of a fresh start, away from the familiar, and come out the other side with a memory of something you have experienced.

woolfolk

Yarn can seem like such a humble thing when it comes into our hands. A single skein, while special, does not seem life altering, but yarn has more power to change and alter a landscape than most people realize. Sheep are notoriously destructive creatures, especially in large numbers. Grazing patterns can strip areas of land miles wide, removing the small vegetation that prevents soil erosion and compromising the soil stability of an area. This can initiate a process called "desertification": the transformation of a once-fertile environment into one that can no longer sustain plant or animal life.

Knitters must keep a keen eye out for sustainability in sourcing if we want wool to survive. Many farmers are making a conscious effort to prevent overgrazing, limiting the sizes of their flocks and choosing environmental stability over short-term profit margins. Through careful planning and research, it is possible for flocks of sheep to coexist with the ecosystems in which they graze. By diversifying the land on which flocks travel and practicing rotational grazing (moving sheep from area to area), shepherds are able to contribute to the natural spread of vegetation, churning soil and fertilizing the areas the sheep travel, encouraging natural biodiversity.

Ovis XXI, a South American cooperative, set about doing exactly this with their Ultimate Merino® project. The grasslands in Patagonia, which straddle Argentina and Chile are some of the most diverse biomes in the world. The co-op focuses on producing the finest ethical wool in this unique area, educating farmers on how to graze their flocks sustainably and contribute to the conservancy of the land. Through careful breeding research and application of high environmental standards, they have managed to create a Merino finer than any other in the world. So fine, in fact, that by touch (and even by microscope) it can be mistaken for cashmere: truly the softest wool available.

When textile lover Kristin Ford heard of the production of this wool, she was quick to see the potential. As the former creative lead at Shibui Knits, an innovative yarn and pattern company well-versed in creating high-end yarns, Kristin knew that the wool was special and expressed her interest to the team at Ovis XXI, forming Woolfolk to spin the yarn in nearby Peru and market it to handknitters, who she knew would appreciate the incredibly soft fiber spun in different ways.

She started with two unique yarns: Tynd, a 2-ply fingering weight, and Får, a chainette plied worsted/aran. The introductory color palette was a minimalist's selection of grays, deep blues, a single dark cranberry, and a few browns. In a knitting world dominated at the time by hand dyers' rainbow applications, Kristin trusted her intuition that these soft, semi-neutral tones would allow the yarn to communicate the cool, soft serenity of the wool's gentle hand. Her architectural background also influenced her decisions in regard to the clean branding and collections of designs released for Woolfolk each year. She works with notably innovative designers who carefully consider the qualities of her ultra-soft staple fibers while expertly crafting them into enviable garments and accessories.

The decidedly un-Argentine names come from Kristin's own Danish cultural heritage, with the company name pulled from her own family tree. Each name is carefully chosen to speak to the yarn itself. Får translates simply to *sheep* while Tynd speaks to the structure—*thin*. New addition Hygge illustrates a broader concept: this brushed bulky-weight wool is named for the feeling of enjoyment that cozy moments bring. Sno, surprisingly, means *twist*, a reference to it being a marled ply version of Tynd.

While at first glance, these yarns may seem simplistic in nature, Kristin has worked to perfect the application and performance of this most luxurious material. Unlike other Merino wools, I have found that Kristin's expert editing has created a yarn that pills less while retaining the supremely soft hand that makes it a delight to knit with. My first project in Får has gone several years without needing much maintenance or de-pilling at all. This is, in and of itself, a true testament to the quality and consideration in regard to this yarn's construction.

Not only does Kristin buy the wool and engineer beautiful yarns, but she also contributes a portion of each sale of Woolfolk to the Ovis XXI foundation, encouraging the production of more Ultimate Merino® and supporting the livelihood of the ranchers involved. You won't find this wool through any other producer— Kristin's relationship with the program involves exclusivity on this fiber for the handknitting market. My hope is that with the encouragement and success of her work, other yarn producers will seek out unique opportunities and preserve these pieces of wool history and innovation for future generations of knitters.

Woolfolk yarn is something every crafter should experience at least once. In combination, the incredible softness of this yarn and carefully chosen spinning methods yield a truly transcendental knitting experience. The feeling is enhanced by the reality that each purchase and use of Woolfolk is part of a bigger, grander picture. Through using this luxurious fiber, knitters are able to touch the lives of ranchers working to make a difference in the way sheep and farmers interact with the environment in Patagonia—all from the comfort of their favorite chair.

Luma

Designed by Véronik Avery

It might feel indulgent to knit with more than a single skein of this ultra-soft Merino at a time, but the best materials surely call for a magnum opus of a knitting project. When designer Véronik Avery asked to make not only a sweater, but a *sweater coat*, with this unique wool, how could I refuse? Being swathed in a cloud-like, lofty layer of Woolfolk Får in a cool white is the ultimate in luxury, and something that I wish each knitter could experience at least once.

Gentle patterned stitches throughout the body allow knitters to focus on the natural beauty of the wool, while reversible cables on the collar add an element of elegant surprise. While the yarn is anything but everyday, this is a garment to live in. Given that each shearing of Ultimate Merino® is limited and dye lots sell out quickly, this textured coat is the knit of a lifetime.

SIZES
X-Small (Small, Medium, Large, X-Large, 2X-Large, 3X-Large)

FINISHED MEASUREMENTS
43 (47, 51, 54½, 58½, 62½, 66)" [109 (119.5, 129.5, 138.5, 148.5, 159, 167.5) cm] bust, with fronts overlapped

YARN
Woolfolk Får [100% Merino wool; 142 yards (130 meters) / 1¾ ounces (50 grams)]: 16 (18, 20, 22, 24, 27, 29) hanks #01 Off White

NEEDLES
Size US 4 (3.5 mm) circular needle 32" (80 cm) long for Tubular CO (optional)

Size US 6 (4 mm) straight needles

Size US 8 (5 mm) straight needles

Spare size US 8 (5 mm) needle, for 3-Needle BO

Change needle size if necessary to obtain correct gauge.

NOTIONS
Cable needle; stitch markers; stitch holders; waste yarn for Tubular CO (optional)

GAUGE
18¾ sts and 32 rows = 4" (10 cm) in Texture Pattern, using larger needles

ABBREVIATIONS
[Inc + k2tog]: With the tip of the left-hand needle inserted from front to back, lift the strand between the 2 needles onto the left-hand needle, then knit it together with next st on left-hand needle.

Dec3R: Slip 3 sts to cn and hold parallel to and behind left-hand needle; *insert right-hand needle into first st on left-hand needle, then into first st on cn; knit these 2 sts together; repeat from * once; insert right-hand needle into first st on cn, then into first st on left-hand needle purlwise; purl these 2 sts together—3 sts decreased.

Dec3L: Slip 3 sts to cn and hold parallel to and in front of left-hand needle; insert right-hand needle into first st on left-hand needle, then into first st on cn purlwise; purl these 2 sts together; *insert right-hand needle into first st on cn, then into first st on left-hand needle; knit these 2 sts together; repeat from * once—3 sts decreased.

SPECIAL TECHNIQUE
3-NEEDLE BO: Place the sts to be joined onto two same-size needles; hold the pieces to be joined with the wrong sides facing each other and the needles parallel, both pointing to the right. Holding both needles in your left hand, and using working yarn and a third needle same size or one size larger, insert third needle into first st on front needle, then into first st on back needle; knit these two sts together; *knit next st from each needle together (2 sts on right-hand needle); pass first st over second st to BO 1 st. Repeat from * until 1 st remains on third needle; cut yarn and fasten off.

LEFT FRONT

Note: If you don't wish to work a Tubular CO, use smaller needles, working yarn, and your preferred method to CO 58 (62, 66, 70, 74, 82, 86) sts, then proceed to Ribbing Set-Up Row 1.

Tubular CO

Using smaller needles, waste yarn, and your preferred method, CO 30 (32, 34, 36, 38, 42, 44) sts. Change to working yarn.

Row 1 (RS): K1, [inc + k2tog], *insert right-hand needle from back to front under strand between needles and purl strand, k1; repeat from * to end—58 (62, 66, 70, 74, 82, 86) sts.

Row 2: P1, k1, *slip 1 wyib, k1; repeat from * to last st, slip 1 wyib.

Row 3: K1, *slip 1 wyib, k1; repeat from * to last st, k1.

Row 4: Repeat Row 2.

With RS facing, rearrange sts as follows (without knitting sts): Slip 1, *slip 2 sts (1 knit st, 1 purl st) to right-hand needle, slip 1 knit st to cn and hold to front, slip 1 purl st to right-hand needle, slip 1 st from cn to right-hand needle; repeat from * to last 13 sts, slip 13 sts in their current order to right-hand needle. Slide sts back to opposite end of needle, ready to work a RS row.

Ribbing Set-Up Row 1 (RS): *K2, p2; repeat from * to last 14 sts, knit to end.

Ribbing Set-Up Row 2: Slip 1 wyif, k11, *p2, k2; repeat from * to last 14 sts, p2, knit to end.

Rows 3–6: Repeat Ribbing Set-Up Rows 1 and 2 twice.

Row 7: *K2, p2; repeat from * to last 38 sts, pm, work Chart A across next 26 sts, pm, knit to end.

Work even for 16 rows.

Change to larger needles.

Texture Set-Up Row 1 (WS): Slip 1 wyif, knit to marker, sm, work to next marker, sm, M1L 0 (0, 1, 0, 0, 0, 0) time(s), knit to last st, M1L 1 (0, 1, 1, 0, 1, 0) time(s), p1—59 (62, 68, 71, 74, 83, 86) sts.

Texture Set-Up Row 2: K1, work Texture Pattern to marker, sm, work to end.

Work even until piece measures approximately 11 (11¼, 11½, 12, 12¼, 12½, 12¾)" [28 (28.5, 29, 30.5, 31, 32, 32.5) cm] from the beginning, ending with Row 2 of Texture Pattern.

Shape Side and Change to Charts B and C

Note: Side shaping will be worked at the same time as changing to Charts B and C; please read entire section through before beginning.

Row 1 (RS): Work to 1 st before marker, [k1, yo, k1] in next st, sm, work to end—2 sts increased.

Row 2: Work even, working increased sts into Texture Pattern.

Row 3: Work to 2 sts before marker, k1-f/b, p1, sm, work to end—1 st increased.

Rows 4–48: Repeat Row 2.

Repeat Rows 1–48 once, then Rows 1–4 once.

AT THE SAME TIME, when piece measures approximately 20¼ (20¼, 20¼, 21¼, 21¼, 21¼, 21¼)" [51.5 (51.5, 51.5, 54, 54, 54, 54) cm] from the beginning, ending with Row 2 of Chart A, change to Chart B between markers; work Rows 1–10 of Chart B once, then Rows 3–8 three times. Change to Chart C between markers; work Rows 1 and 2 of Chart C once—74 (77, 83, 86, 89, 98, 101) sts. Piece should measure approximately 25 (25, 25, 26, 26, 26, 26)" [63.5 (63.5, 63.5, 66, 66, 66, 66) cm]. Make note of last row of Texture Pattern worked.

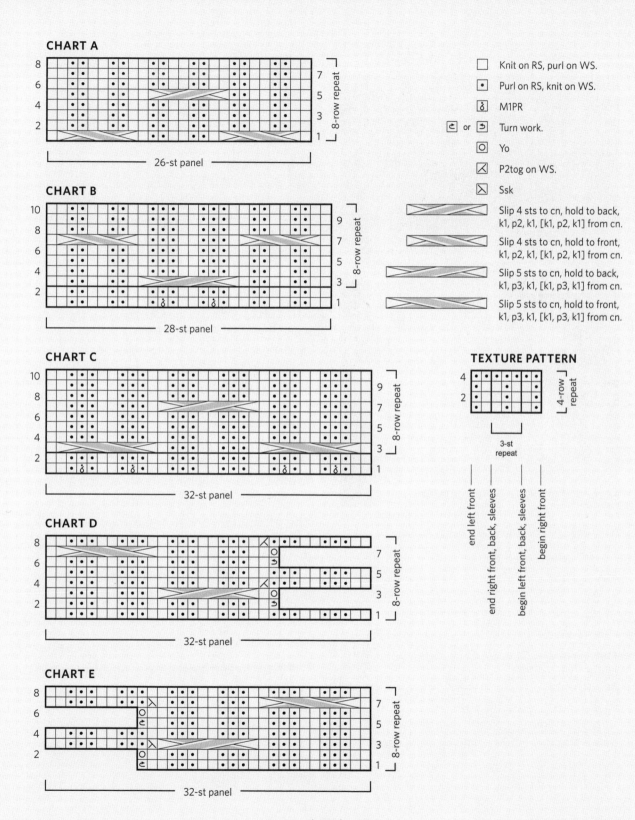

Shape Raglan Armhole

Working Rows 3–10 of Chart C throughout remainder of raglan, BO 3 (3, 6, 9, 9, 12, 12) sts at armhole edge once, then decrease 3 sts on next RS row, then every 4 rows 4 (5, 5, 4, 4, 8, 8) times, then every 8 rows 2 (2, 3, 4, 5, 3, 4) times as follows: Work 3 sts, dec3L, work to end—50 sts remain.

Next Row (WS): Work to 1 st before last marker, pm, work 1 st, remove marker, work to end.

Decrease 1 st on next RS row, then every other row 4 times, as follows: Work to 2 sts before marker, k2tog, work to end—45 sts remain.

Work even until armhole measures approximately 7¼ (8¼, 9¼, 9¼, 10¼, 10¼, 11¼)" [18.5 (21, 23.5, 23.5, 26, 26, 28.5) cm], ending with Row 4 of Chart C.

Shape Collar

Set-Up Row (RS): K1, sm, work Chart D to marker, work to end.

Work even until you have completed Rows 1–8 of Chart D seven times, then work even for 0 (2, 2, 4, 4, 4, 6) more rows. Transfer sts to holder.

RIGHT FRONT

Note: *If you don't wish to work a Tubular CO, use smaller needles, working yarn, and your preferred method to CO 58 (62, 66, 70, 74, 82, 86) sts, then proceed to Ribbing Set-Up Row 1.*

Tubular CO

Work as for Left Front through Row 4 of Tubular CO—58 (62, 66, 70, 74, 82, 86) sts after Row 2.

With RS facing, rearrange sts as follows (without knitting sts): Slip 13 sts in their current order to right-hand needle, *slip 2 sts (1 knit st, 1 purl st) to right-hand needle, slip 1 knit st to cn and hold to front, slip 1 purl st to right-hand needle, slip 1 st from cn to right-hand needle; repeat from * to last st, slip 1 st to right-hand needle. Slide sts back to opposite end of needle, ready to work a RS row.

Ribbing Set-Up Row 1 (RS): Slip 1 wyif, k13, *p2, k2; repeat from * to end.

Ribbing Set-Up Row 2: P2, *k2, p2; repeat from * to last 12 sts, knit to end.

Rows 3–6: Repeat Ribbing Set-Up Rows 1 and 2 twice.

Row 7: Slip 1 wyif, k11, pm, work Chart A across next 26 sts, pm, work to end.

Work even for 16 rows.

Change to larger needles.

Texture Set-Up Row 1 (WS): P1, M1L 1 (0, 1, 1, 0, 1, 0) time(s), knit to marker, M1L 0 (0, 1, 0, 0, 0, 0) time(s), sm, work to next marker, sm, knit to end—59 (62, 68, 71, 74, 83, 86) sts.

Texture Set-Up Row 2: Slip 1 wyif, k11, sm, work to next marker, sm, work Texture Pattern to last st, k1.

Work even until piece measures approximately 11 (11¼, 11½, 12, 12¼, 12½, 12¾)" [28 (28.5, 29, 30.5, 31, 32, 32.5) cm] from the beginning, ending with Row 2 of Texture Pattern.

Shape Side and Change to Charts B and C

Note: Side shaping will be worked at the same time as changing to Charts B and C; please read entire section through before beginning.

Row 1 (RS): Work to second marker, sm, [k1, yo, k1] in next st, work to end—2 sts increased.

Row 2: Work even, working increased sts into Texture Pattern.

Row 3: Work to second marker, sm, p1, k1-f/b, work to end—1 st increased.

Rows 4–48: Repeat Row 2.

Repeat Rows 1–48 once, then Rows 1–4 once.

AT THE SAME TIME, when piece measures approximately 20¼ (20¼, 20¼, 21¼, 21¼, 21¼, 21¼)" [51.5 (51.5, 51.5, 54, 54, 54, 54) cm] from the beginning, ending with Row 2 of Chart A, change to Chart B between markers; work Rows 1–10 of Chart B once, then Rows 3–8 three times. Change to Chart C between markers; work Rows 1–3 of Chart C once— 74 (77, 83, 86, 89, 98, 101) sts. Piece should measure approximately 25 (25, 25, 26, 26, 26, 26)" [63.5 (63.5, 63.5, 66, 66, 66, 66) cm].

Shape Raglan Armhole

Working Rows 4–10 of Chart C once, then Rows 3–8 of chart throughout remainder of raglan, BO 3 (3, 6, 9, 9, 12, 12) sts at armhole edge once, then decrease 3 sts on next RS row, then every 4 rows 4 (5, 5, 4, 4, 8, 8) times, then every 8 rows 2 (2, 3, 4, 5, 3, 4) times as follows: Work to last 9 sts, dec3R, work to end—50 sts remain.

Next Row (WS): Work 6 sts, remove marker, work 1 st, pm, work to end.

Decrease 1 st this row, then every other row 4 times, as follows: Work to marker, ssk, work to end—45 sts remain.

Work even until armhole measures approximately 7¼ (8¼, 9¼, 9¼, 10¼, 10¼, 11¼)" [18.5 (21, 23.5, 23.5, 26, 26, 28.5) cm], ending with Row 4 of Chart C.

Shape Collar

Set-Up Row (RS): Work to marker, sm, work Chart E to marker, sm, k1.

Work even until you have completed Rows 1–8 of Chart E seven times.

Set-Up Row (RS): Work to marker, sm, work Chart C (beginning with Row 5) to marker, sm, k1.

Work even for 3 (1, 1, 5, 3, 7, 7) row(s). Transfer sts to holder; do not cut yarn.

BACK

Note: If you don't wish to work a Tubular CO, use smaller needles, working yarn, and your preferred method to CO 98 (110, 118, 126, 134, 146, 154) sts, then proceed to Ribbing Set-Up Row 1.

Tubular CO

Using smaller needles, waste yarn, and your preferred method, CO 50 (56, 60, 64, 68, 74, 78) sts. Change to working yarn.

Work Rows 1–4 of Tubular CO as for Left Front—98 (110, 118, 126, 134, 146, 154) sts after Row 2.

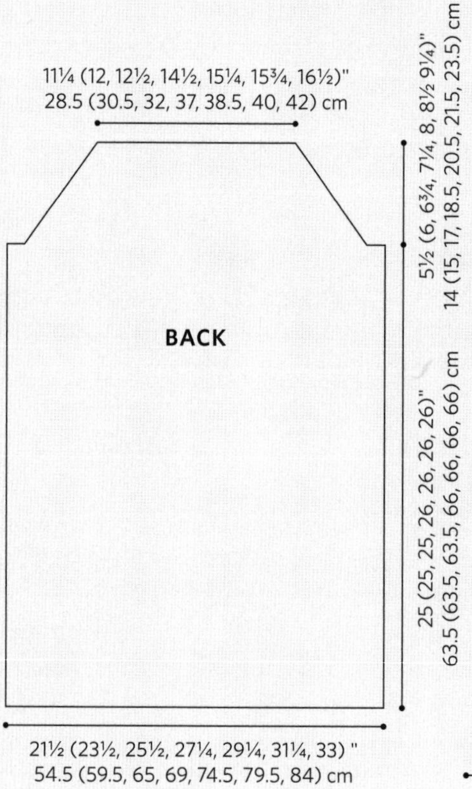
11¼ (12, 12½, 14½, 15¼, 15¾, 16½)"
28.5 (30.5, 32, 37, 38.5, 40, 42) cm
5½ (6, 6¾, 7¼, 8, 8½ 9¼)"
14 (15, 17, 18.5, 20.5, 21.5, 23.5) cm
BACK
25 (25, 25, 26, 26, 26, 26)"
63.5 (63.5, 63.5, 66, 66, 66, 66) cm
21½ (23½, 25½, 27¼, 29¼, 31¼, 33) "
54.5 (59.5, 65, 69, 74.5, 79.5, 84) cm

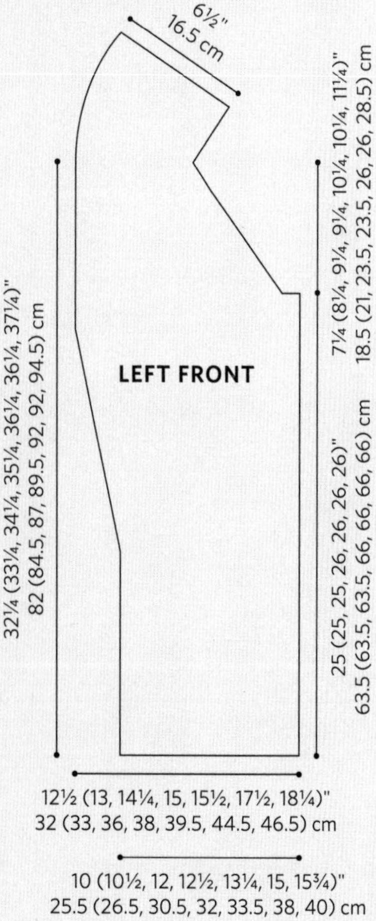
6½"
16.5 cm
32¼ (33¼, 34¼, 35¼, 36¼, 36¼, 37¼)"
82 (84.5, 87, 89.5, 92, 92, 94.5) cm
LEFT FRONT
7¼ (8¼, 9¼, 9¼, 10¼, 10¼, 11¼)"
18.5 (21, 23.5, 23.5, 26, 26, 28.5) cm
25 (25, 25, 26, 26, 26, 26)"
63.5 (63.5, 63.5, 66, 66, 66, 66) cm
12½ (13, 14¼, 15, 15½, 17½, 18¼)"
32 (33, 36, 38, 39.5, 44.5, 46.5) cm
10 (10½, 12, 12½, 13¼, 15, 15¾)"
25.5 (26.5, 30.5, 32, 33.5, 38, 40) cm

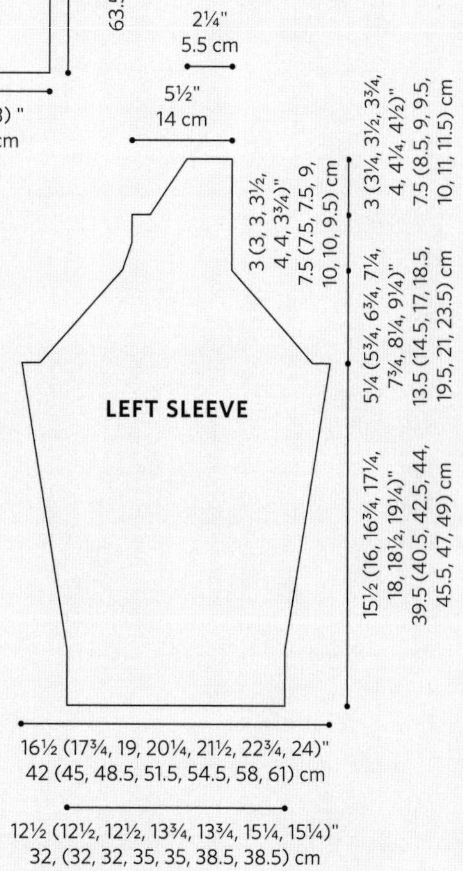
2¼"
5.5 cm
5½"
14 cm
3 (3, 3, 3½, 4, 4, 3¾)"
7.5 (7.5, 7.5, 9, 10, 10, 9.5) cm
3 (3¼, 3½, 3¾, 4, 4¼, 4½)"
7.5 (8.5, 9, 9.5, 10, 11, 11.5) cm
5¼ (5¾, 6¾, 7¼, 7¾, 8¼, 9¼)"
13.5 (14.5, 17, 18.5, 19.5, 21, 23.5) cm
LEFT SLEEVE
15½ (16, 16¾, 17¼, 18, 18½, 19¼)"
39.5 (40.5, 42.5, 44, 45.5, 47, 49) cm
16½ (17¾, 19, 20¼, 21½, 22¾, 24)"
42 (45, 48.5, 51.5, 54.5, 58, 61) cm
12½ (12½, 12½, 13¾, 13¾, 15¼, 15¼)"
32, (32, 32, 35, 35, 38.5, 38.5) cm

With RS facing, rearrange sts as follows (without knitting sts): Slip 1 st, *slip 2 sts (1 knit st, 1 purl st) to right-hand needle, slip 1 knit st to cn and hold to front, slip 1 purl st to right-hand needle, slip 1 st from cn to right-hand needle; repeat from * to last st, slip 1 to right-hand needle. Slide sts back to opposite end of needle, ready to work a RS row.

Ribbing Set-Up Row 1 (RS): *K2, p2; repeat from * to last 14 sts, knit to end.

Ribbing Set-Up Row 2: Slip 1 wyif, k11, *p2, k2; repeat from * to last 14 sts, p2, knit to end.

Rows 3–6: Repeat Ribbing Set-Up Rows 1 and 2 twice.

Row 7: *K2, p2; repeat from * to last 38 sts, pm, work Chart A across next 26 sts, pm, knit to end.

Work even for 16 rows.

Change to larger needles.

Texture Set-Up Row 1 (WS): P1, knit to last st, increasing 3 (0, 1, 2, 3, 0, 1) st(s) evenly across, p1—101 (110, 119, 128, 137, 146, 155) sts.

Texture Set-Up Row 2: K1, work Texture Pattern to last st, k1.

Work even until piece measures same as for Left Front to armhole shaping, ending with same row of Texture Pattern as for Left Front.

Shape Raglan Armholes

BO 3 (3, 6, 9, 9, 12, 12) sts at beginning of next 2 rows— 95 (104, 107, 110, 119, 122, 131) sts remain.

Decrease 3 sts each side this row, then every 4 rows 3 (4, 2, 0, 0, 0, 0) times, then every 8 rows 3 (3, 5, 5, 7, 6, 7) times, then every 12 rows 0 (0, 0, 1, 0, 1, 1) time(s), as follows: Work 3 sts, dec3L, work to last 9 sts, dec3R, work to end—53 (56, 59, 68, 71, 74, 77) sts remain.

Work even until armholes measure 5½ (6, 6¾, 7¼, 8, 8½, 9¼)" [14 (15, 17, 18.5, 20.5, 21.5, 23.5) cm].
BO all sts.

LEFT SLEEVE

Note: If you don't wish to work a Tubular CO, use smaller needles, working yarn, and your preferred method to CO 58 (58, 58, 62, 62, 70, 70) sts, then work as for Back to end of ribbing.

Tubular CO

Using smaller needles, waste yarn, and your preferred method, CO 30 (30, 30, 32, 32, 36, 36) sts. Change to working yarn.

Work as for Back to end of ribbing—58 (58, 58, 62, 62, 70, 70) sts after Row 2.

Texture Set-Up Row 1 (WS): P1, knit to last st, increasing 1 (1, 1, 3, 3, 1, 1) st(s) evenly across, p1—59 (59, 59, 65, 65, 71, 71) sts.

Texture Set-Up Row 2: K1, work Texture Pattern to last st, k1.

Work even until piece measures 4" (10 cm) from the beginning, ending with a WS row.

Shape Sleeve

Increase 1 st each side on this row, then every 12 (8, 8, 8, 8, 8, 6) rows 1 (11, 5, 7, 1, 3, 18) time(s), then every 10 (0, 6, 6, 6, 6, 4) rows 7 (0, 9, 7, 16, 14, 2) times, as follows: K1, M1R, work to last st, M1L, k1—77 (83, 89, 95, 101, 107, 113) sts.

Work even until piece measures 15½ (16, 16¾, 17¼, 18, 18½, 19¼) [39.5 (40.5, 42.5, 44, 45.5, 47, 49) cm] from the beginning, ending with a WS row.

Shape Raglan Cap

BO 3 (3, 6, 9, 9, 12, 12) sts at beginning of next 2 rows, then decrease 3 sts each side on next RS row, then every 4 rows 2 (3, 1, 0, 1, 0, 0) time(s), then every 8 rows 4 (4, 6, 7, 7, 8, 9) times, as follows: Work 3 sts, dec3L, work to last 9 sts, dec3R, work to end—29 sts remain.

Work even for 9 rows.

Shape Front Edge

Next Row (RS): Work to last 9 sts, dec3R, work to end—26 sts remain.

Work even until cap measures approximately 8¼ (8¾, 9¾, 10¾, 11¾, 12¼, 13)" [21 (22, 25, 27.5, 30, 31, 33) cm], ending with Row 1 of Texture Pattern.

Shape Neck Edge

Next Row (WS): BO 6 sts, work to end—20 sts remain.

Decrease 3 sts at neck edge on next RS row, then every 4 rows twice, as follows: Work to last 9 sts, dec3R, work to end—11 sts remain.

Work even until cap measures 11¼ (12, 13¼, 14½, 15¾, 16½, 17½)" [28.5 (30.5, 33.5, 37, 40, 42, 44.5) cm], ending with a WS row. Cut yarn, leaving a long tail, and place all sts on holder.

RIGHT SLEEVE

Work as for Left Sleeve to *Shape Front Edge.*

Shape Front Edge

Next Row (RS): Work 3 sts, dec3L, work to end—26 sts remain.

Work even until cap measures approximately 8¼ (8¾, 9¾, 10¾, 11¾, 12¼, 13)" [21 (22, 25, 27.5, 30, 31, 33) cm], ending with Row 4 of Texture Pattern.

Shape Neck Edge

Next Row (RS): BO 6 sts, work to end—20 sts rem.

Work even for 1 row.

Decrease 3 sts at neck edge on next RS row, then every 4 rows twice, as follows: Work 3 sts, dec3L, work to end—11 sts remain.

Work even until cap measures 11¼ (12, 13¼, 14½, 15¾, 16½, 17½)" [28.5 (30.5, 33.5, 37, 40, 42, 44.5) cm], ending with a WS row. Cut yarn, leaving a long tail, and place all sts on holder.

FINISHING

Block pieces as desired.

Sew raglan edge of each Sleeve to raglan edge of Back (making sure to sew Left Sleeve to left armhole and Right Sleeve to right armhole), then sew straight side edge of top of Sleeve to Back BO edge, adding or removing rows at top of Sleeve to meet at center Back and using 1 live st from top of Sleeve in seam; leave remaining sts on holders. Sew raglan edge of each Front to raglan edge of each Sleeve, then sew straight side edge of top of Front to Sleeve, adding or removing rows at top of Front to meet at center Back and using 1 live st from both Front and Sleeve in seam; leave remaining sts on holders. Transfer sts from Right Sleeve and Front holders to one needle and sts from Left Sleeve and Front holders to second needle; with WSs of pieces together (seam will be on RS), join sts using 3-Needle BO. Sew side and Sleeve seams.

m Yak

In creative industries, we often speak about passion. Passion for craft, passion for materials, passion for the process. Passion has become synonymous for many with craftsmanship, or research, or taking the time to learn something properly. The definition of passion, though, is a strong and barely controllable emotion. Passion is drive—and being passionate about something keeps us moving toward our goals, even when they seem unattainable or inaccessible. All too often, people assume that having a passion for something traditionally related to a hobby industry is a luxury, and that those who are able to pursue careers related to crafts have some special privileges that allow them to do so. This is not usually the case. Often, those who work in a field they are passionate about fight to get there by doing the unexpected and not letting the world push them into boxes. Paola Vanza of mYak is one of those people.

Paola grew up in a small, 3,000-person Italian village where the expectation of young women was to marry locally and have a beautiful, simple life. Gripped by wanderlust, Paola announced that she was going to do something almost unthinkable—she was going to leave town to attend university, and then study Chinese. She moved to Tibet in the 1990s and immediately fell in love with the culture, so entirely different from her own.

During her studies in China, she had the opportunity to explore the nomadic cultures of Tibet. Much like native North American cultures,

Tibetan culture has evolved over time to center around a single animal: the yak. Each yak is precious to the families that care for it. The animal produces milk, which can be turned into cheese and yogurt. The dung becomes a fuel that provides fire and warmth. The luxurious dual coat of the yak is used for many textiles; the rough guard hairs are woven into tent fabrics, while the softer down is used for garments. The animal also provides a source of meat. When Paola was visiting Tibet, the yak herders were looking for other ways to turn their beloved animals into a source of income, to provide their families with better medical and dental care, among other modern conveniences.

Paola joined forces with other researchers there to tackle this problem. Andrea Dominici, a veterinarian who had gone to Tibet to research yaks, had gotten to know families in the community intimately, and together with Paola, she shared a desire to help these people earn a modern-day living while sustaining their existing traditions and way of life. While tending the baby yaks, they noticed that the down from the animals was much softer than that of the adults. Paola returned to Italy, suitcase laden with yak fiber samples, and took advantage of Italy's rich history in her own way, visiting spinning mills and developing yarns with this new fiber. The mills were amazed at the initial results—baby yak down, similar to cashmere in texture and softness, would be a great offering for the fashion and hobbyist knitting industries alike. With

an average micron count of 17, many a knitter would be delighted to have a skein in their luxury yarn stash.

Paola returned to Tibet and worked with Andrea to teach the Tibetans to efficiently harvest the fiber in a way that would result in the best yarns. Baby yaks do not require shearing—their summer coat falls off. So, through the course of regular grooming, the fiber can be collected and guard hairs can be removed by hand. Every spring, Paola and Andrea visit Tibet, paying cash in advance for fiber purchased from the co-op that has been set up for mYak. In midsummer they check on the quality and make sure the fiber is washed and vegetation removed before it gets sent to Italy. mYak is not blended or mixed with low-grade fibers and is dehaired as close to Tibet as possible to lower the environmental impact associated with shipping. The fiber is then sent on to Italy, where it is milled into yarns in both the common chocolate-brown shade and rarer pale shades.

While Paola does overdye the darker shades (and lighter ones, too), she does not encourage the farmers to work toward breeding paler animals. She is not out to change the culture, only to support it, and too much interference in this area could result in programs that would change the Tibetan way of life. The preservation of culture and ethical treatment of those who produce the fiber is the most important driving force for her. She utilizes no middlemen, working directly with the co-op of farmers to source, ship, and process the fiber. Her production is not cheap, and neither is the yarn, but that is a sacrifice both she and her customers are willing to make for quality fiber. The yarn, carded and not combed, is warm, light, and has a delightful bloom with a slight sheen.

Now residing in New York, Paola cherishes her trips back to Italy and Tibet. While she lives in one of the most populous cities in the world, in her own words, her mind and heart have always been somewhere else—somewhere small, where community matters, and tradition, culture, and family are the greatest treasures. In that way, she has never left home at all.

Rhodiola

Designed by Michele Wang

Sometimes a special yarn needs only the simplest of stitches to truly celebrate what makes it unique. Michele Wang's pullover makes use of Stockinette and textured tweed stitch to showcase the beautiful and unique texture of 100 percent baby yak down. The natural color is used throughout the top portion of the body in a pale oatmeal hue, while the hem utilizes the darker, more common brown of yak fiber, overdyed to a rich, slightly heathered navy. Try not to be lured by the speed of bulky stitches and larger needles, and take the time to treat this knit as meditative, giving each stitch the attention it deserves.

SIZES
Small (Medium, Large, 1X-Large, 2X-Large)

FINISHED MEASUREMENTS
36 (41½, 44, 48½, 52)" [91.5 (105.5, 112, 123, 132) cm] bust

YARN
mYak Baby Yak Chunky [100% baby yak; 65 yards (59 meters) / 1¾ ounces / 50 grams]: 9 (10, 11, 12, 14) hanks [565 (630, 710, 780, 855) yards / 515 (575, 650, 715, 780) meters] Desert (MC); 3 (3, 4, 4, 4) hanks [170 (185, 215, 240, 250) yards / 155 (170, 195, 220, 230) meters] Midnight Blue (A)

NEEDLES
One pair size US 10½ (6.5 mm) straight needles

One pair size US 10 (6 mm) straight needles

One size US 10 (6 mm) circular needle 16" (40 cm) long

Spare size US 10 (6 mm) circular needle 16" (40 cm) long or longer, for Tubular BO (optional)

Change needle size if necessary to obtain correct gauge.

NOTIONS
Waste yarn for Tubular CO (optional); stitch marker

GAUGE
14 sts and 19 rows = 4" (10 cm) in St st, using larger needles

STITCH PATTERNS

1X1 RIB FLAT
(even number of sts; 1-row repeat)
Row 1 (RS): K2, *p1, k1; repeat from * to end.
Row 2: Knit the knit sts and purl the purl sts as they face you.
Repeat Row 2 for 1x1 Rib Flat.

1X1 RIB IN THE ROUND
(even number of sts; 1-rnd repeat)
All Rnds: *K1, p1; repeat from * to end.

TWEED STITCH
(odd number of sts; 4-row repeat)
Row 1 (RS): Using MC, k1, *slip 1, k1; repeat from * to end.
Row 2: P2, *k1, p1; repeat from * to last st, p1.
Row 3: Using A, k2, *slip 1, k1; repeat from * to last st, k1.
Row 4: P1, *k1, p1; repeat from * to end.
Repeat Rows 1–4 for Tweed Stitch.

SPECIAL TECHNIQUES

TUBULAR CO (optional)

Using waste yarn and Backward Loop CO (see Special Techniques, page 167), CO the number of sts indicated. Change to A.

Row 1 (RS): K2, *yo, k1; repeat from * to end.
Row 2: Slip 1 wyif, *k1, slip 1 wyif; repeat from * to last st, slip 1 wyif.
Row 3: K2, *slip 1 wyif, k1; repeat from * to end.
Row 4: *P1, k1; repeat from * to last 2 sts, p2.

Continue as instructed.

TUBULAR BO (optional)

Set-Up Rnd 1: *K1, slip 1 wyif; repeat from * to end.
Set-Up Rnd 2: *Slip 1 wyib, p1; repeat from * to end.

Separate knit and purl stitches, as follows: *Slip 1 (knit stitch) to front needle, slip 1 (purl stitch) to back needle; repeat from * until all sts have been separated. Graft stitches on front needle to stitches on back needle using Kitchener stitch.

KITCHENER STITCH (optional)

Using a blunt tapestry needle, thread a length of yarn approximately 4 times the length of the section to be joined. Hold the pieces to be joined wrong sides together, with the needles holding the sts parallel, both ends pointing to the right. Working from right to left, insert tapestry needle into first st on front needle as if to purl, pull yarn through, leaving st on needle; insert tapestry needle into first st on back needle as if to knit, pull yarn through, leaving st on needle; *insert tapestry needle into first st on front needle as if to knit, pull yarn through, remove st from needle; insert tapestry needle into next st on front needle as if to purl, pull yarn through, leave st on needle; insert tapestry needle into first st on back needle as if to purl, pull yarn through, remove st from needle; insert tapestry needle into next st on back needle as if to knit, pull yarn through, leave st on needle. Repeat from *, working 3 or 4 sts at a time, then go back and adjust tension to match the pieces being joined. When 1 st remains on each needle, cut yarn and pass through last 2 sts to fasten off.

PATTERN NOTES

You may substitute your preferred cast-on for the Tubular CO called for in the pattern. Simply use A to cast on the number of sts that are indicated after the completion of the Tubular CO.

You may use your preferred stretchy bind-off for the neckband instead of the Tubular BO.

BACK

Using smaller needles, waste yarn, and Tubular CO, CO 33 (38, 40, 44, 47) sts. When Tubular CO instructions are complete, you will have 64 (74, 78, 86, 92) sts on the needle.

Begin 1x1 Rib; work even until piece measures 2½" (6.5 cm) from the beginning, ending with a WS row, and decreasing 1 st on final row—63 (73, 77, 85, 91) sts remain.

Change to larger needles and Tweed st; work even until piece measures 6½" (16.5 cm) from the beginning, ending with a WS row.

Change to St st and MC; work even until piece measures 16½ (16½, 17, 17½, 18)" [42 (42, 43, 44.5, 45.5) cm] from the beginning, ending with a WS row.

Shape Armholes

BO 4 (5, 5, 6, 7) sts at beginning of next 2 rows, 3 sts at beginning of next 2 rows, then 1 st at beginning of next 4 (4, 4, 6, 8) rows—45 (53, 57, 61, 63) sts remain.

Work even until armholes measure 7¼ (7¾, 8¼, 8½, 9)" [18.5 (19.5, 21, 21.5, 23) cm], ending with a WS row.

Shape Shoulders

Using Sloped BO (see Special Techniques, page 167), BO 5 (6, 7, 7, 8) sts at beginning of next 4 (4, 4, 2, 2) rows, then 0 (0, 0, 8, 8) sts at beginning of next 0 (0, 0, 2, 2) rows.

BO remaining 25 (29, 29, 31, 31) sts.

FRONT

Work as for Back until armholes measure 4¾ (5¼, 5¾, 6, 6½)" [12 (13.5, 14.5, 15, 16.5) cm], ending with a WS row—45 (53, 57, 61, 63) sts remain.

Shape Neck

Work 19 (22, 24, 25, 26) sts, join a second ball of yarn, BO center 7 (9, 9, 11, 11) sts, and work to end.

Working both sides at the same time, BO 3 sts at each neck edge 1 (2, 2, 2, 2) time(s), 2 sts 2 (1, 1, 1, 1) time(s), then 1 st twice—10 (12, 14, 15, 16) sts remain each side.

Shape Shoulders

BO 5 (6, 7, 7, 8) sts at each armhole edge 2 (2, 2, 1, 1) time(s), then 0 (0, 0, 8, 8) sts 0 (0, 0, 1, 1) time(s).

SLEEVES

Using smaller needles, waste yarn, and Tubular CO, CO 16 (16, 17, 18, 19) sts. When Tubular CO instructions are complete, you will have 30 (30, 32, 34, 36) sts on the needle.

Begin 1x1 Rib; work even until piece measures 2½" (6.5 cm) from the beginning, ending with a WS row.

Change to larger needles, MC, and St st; work even for 2 rows.

Shape Sleeve

Increase Row (RS): Increase 1 st each side this row, then every 10 (10, 8, 8, 6) rows 1 (6, 3, 8, 4) time(s), then every 12 (0, 10, 0, 8) rows 4 (0, 4, 0, 5) times, as follows: K2, M1L, knit to last 2 sts, M1R, k2—42 (44, 48, 52, 56) sts.

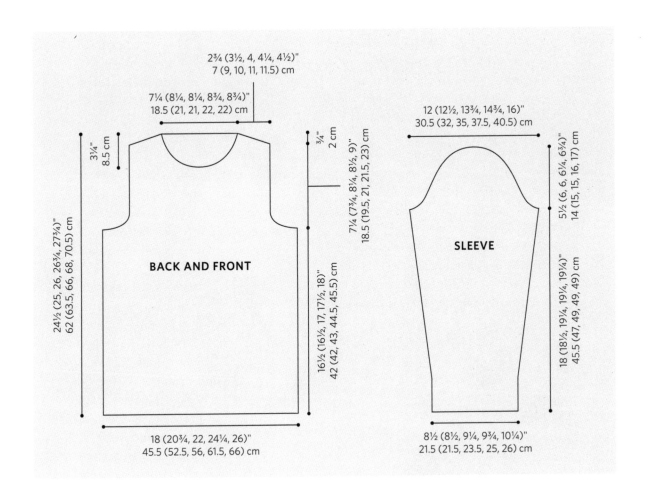

Work even until piece measures 18 (18½, 19¼, 19¼, 19¼)" [45.5 (47, 49, 49, 49) cm] from the beginning, ending with a WS row.

Shape Cap

BO 4 (5, 5, 6, 7) sts at beginning of next 2 rows, 3 (1, 3, 3, 2) st(s) at beginning of next 2 (24, 2, 2, 2) rows, 1 (2, 1, 1, 1) st(s) at beginning of next 20 (2, 22, 24, 26) rows, then 2 (0, 2, 2, 3) sts at beginning of next 2 (0, 2, 2, 2) rows. BO remaining 4 (6, 6, 6, 6) sts.

FINISHING

Block pieces as desired. Sew shoulder seams. Set in Sleeves; sew side and Sleeve seams.

Neckband

With RS facing, using circular needle and A, and beginning at right shoulder, pick up and knit 25 (29, 29, 31, 31) sts along Back neck edge, then 37 (39, 39, 41, 41) sts along Front neck edge—62 (68, 68, 72, 72) sts. Join for working in the rnd; pm for beginning of rnd. Work in 1x1 Rib for 1" (2.5 cm). BO all sts using Tubular BO.

YARN /for/ THOUGHT

wanderlust

Sometimes, a yarn line is defining to a region. Textiles have long been a commodity that can support and sustain cultures, and many of the fibers available to yarn enthusiasts have a mission behind them to provide fair trade income or rescue a disappearing industry. By purchasing these yarns, we not only get to contribute to our own enjoyment of a single project, but also to the ability of individuals elsewhere in the world to provide for their families. "Feel-good" fiber purchases are not just lip service; they offer a connection to the fiber traditions of other countries and cultures. Here are a few other options for you to explore on your knitting journey.

HABU TEXTILES

Well known for innovative techniques and textures, Habu Textiles has a yarn line that challenges many knitters to reach beyond traditional materials to try something new. Moldable cobweb-thin wire, raffia, paper, banana fiber, ramie, rayon, hemp, and silk are imagined anew with minimalist, fashion-forward patterns. These fibers encourage us to break the mold of what we consider "knitting-suitable yarns." Perhaps most intriguing is the way that owner and operator Takako Ueki has managed to convey her Japanese culture within the yarn's packaging and presence; each bundle or cone seems to simultaneously straddle the idea of textile history and present-day innovation.

KNIT COLLAGE

I'm sure that many of you are surprised to see a novelty yarn featured in this book, but trust me, Knit Collage has earned their place. Amy Small's hand-spun brand is whimsical, magical, and fun. The yarns are spun entirely in Punjab, India, where Amy hires women and teaches them how to spin, card, and prepare the small edgings, ribbons, and tassels that are worked into each skein.

Her brand provides a livelihood for these women and inspiration for crafters all over the world. The jovial thick and thin textures of some of my favorite Knit Collage yarns perfectly embody Amy's own personality. Even if you aren't quite ready to embrace the embellishments, you can get the full experience with subtly spun Sister, which comes in solids but also in lovely, naturally heathered tones.

JONES & VANDERMEER

The team at Jones & Vandermeer takes pride in finding the unusual and exotic. Like 1700s-era explorers who traveled around the world to bring back unusual spices and silks, they seek out unique fibers and yarns for their online boutique store. One of their more unusual fibers is Happy Mink, which uses a blend of cashmere and hand-combed mink fiber. These fibers are then spun by hand into 120-yard (110-m) hanks perfect for a small project meant to spoil the wearer. I particularly love this yarn for gifts. Although indulgent, I've found that gifting someone a garment made in such a strange, fine fiber also gifts them with the story of where it comes from.

beyond
slow knitting

SLOW KNITTING ISN'T JUST A movement or a lifestyle. It's a conscientious choice to respect our materials and the people who make them, but also to respect ourselves and the time we devote to the hobby we adore. Any knitter, of any skill level, age, or income, can adopt slow knitting as their own.

For those who are just beginning their knitting journey, embracing slow knitting is an opportunity to carefully curate a yarn collection that will be loved throughout the process. By learning about our materials and notions before purchasing them, it's possible to make decisions that influence what may be available for future crafters. You have the opportunity to cast on projects that you are passionate about from the start, and never spend time knitting anything you don't enjoy.

Passionate knitters fully absorbed in the craft will find that slow knitting practices may encourage you to tackle new things. Through exploration, you can remain enthusiastic in the discovery of new yarns and new techniques, and attain the inspiration you need to keep moving through difficult projects. This continual learning process is what often leads individuals both to and away from knitting. By educating ourselves about what we're making, asking ourselves why, and continuing to ask how things we use come into our possession, we can continue the wonder and excitement of those first few moments of knitting.

For knitters who have long practiced this craft, I hope that slow knitting brings a fresh look or validates what you have already come to know on your own. Perhaps it will help release you from the burden of a stash you do not love every part of, a project that has been long-lingering in your basket, or the guilt of the holiday knitting rush. This movement encourages us to be better stewards of the craft we practice, to help preserve it for generations of knitters after us, and to honor those who have come before.

Knitting is a small thing, but it is not simple—each time that we draw wool back from the wheel, bring yarn around the needle to make a stitch, or pin down the corner of a finished garment, we are touching thousands of lives. The lives of knitters who have come before us: family, friends, and craftspeople. The lives of those who have moved herds of fiber animals across the land, who have woken up in the middle of a February evening to tend to a lambing, who have expertly sheared a sheep. The lives of those animals themselves. This craft is not a lonely one, but one as warm and alive as the garments we make. It is meant to be worn, meant to be shared, and meant to be gifted. It is a meditation, a passion, and a necessity.

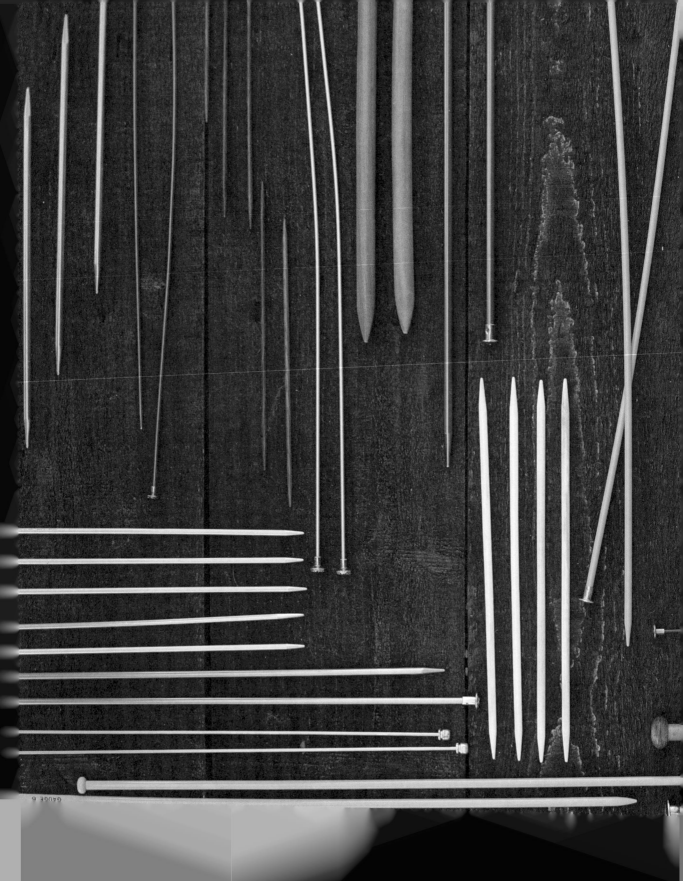

ABBREVIATIONS

BO – Bind off

Cn – Cable needle

CO – Cast on

K1-f/b – Knit into the front loop and back loop of the same stitch to increase 1 stitch.

K2tog – Knit 2 stitches together

K3tog – Knit 3 stitches together

K – Knit

LLI (left lifted increase) – Pick up the stitch two rows below the last stitch on the right-hand needle, picking up from the top down into the back of the stitch, and place on the left-hand needle; knit the picked-up stitch through the front loop to increase 1 stitch.

M1 or M1L (make 1-left slanting) – With the tip of the left-hand needle inserted from front to back, lift the strand between the 2 needles onto the left-hand needle; knit the strand through the back loop to increase 1 stitch.

M1PL (make 1 purlwise-left slanting) – With the tip of the left-hand needle inserted from front to back, lift the strand between the 2 needles onto the left-hand needle; purl the strand through the back loop to increase 1 stitch.

M1PR (make 1 purlwise-right slanting) – With the tip of the left-hand needle inserted from back to front, lift the strand between the 2 needles onto the left-hand needle; purl the strand through the front loop to increase 1 stitch.

M1R (make 1-right slanting) – With the tip of the left-hand needle inserted from back to front, lift the strand between the 2 needles onto the left-hand needle; knit the strand through the front loop to increase 1 stitch.

P2tog – Purl 2 stitches together

Pm – Place marker

P – Purl

Rnd(s) – Round(s)

RLI (right lifted increase) – Pick up the stitch below the next stitch on the left-hand needle, picking up from the bottom up into the back of the stitch, and place it on the left-hand needle; knit the picked-up stitch through the front loop to increase 1 stitch.

RS – Right side

S2kp2 – Slip the next 2 stitches together to the right-hand needle as if to knit 2 together, k1, pass the 2 slipped stitches over.

Sk2p (double decrease) – Slip the next stitch knitwise to the right-hand needle, k2tog, pass the slipped stitch over the stitch from the k2tog.

Sm – Slip marker

Ssk (slip, slip, knit) – Slip the next 2 stitches to the right-hand needle one at a time as if to knit; return them to the left-hand needle one at a time in their new orientation; knit them together through the back loops.

Sssk – Same as ssk, but worked on the next 3 stitches.

Ssp (slip, slip, purl) – Slip the next 2 stitches to the right-hand needle one at a time as if to knit; return them to the left-hand needle one at a time in their new orientation; purl them together through the back loops.

Sssp – Same as ssp, but worked on the next 3 stitches.

St(s) – Stitch(es)

St st – Stockinette stitch

Tbl – Through the back loop

WS – Wrong side

W&t – Wrap and turn

Wyib – With yarn in back

Wyif – With yarn in front

Yo – Yarnover

SPECIAL TECHNIQUES

Backward Loop CO – Make a loop (using a slip knot) with the working yarn and place it on the right-hand needle (first st CO), *wind yarn around thumb clockwise, insert right-hand needle into the front of the loop on thumb, remove thumb and tighten st on needle; repeat from * for remaining sts to be CO, or for casting on at the end of a row in progress.

Long-Tail CO – Leaving tail with about 1" (2.5 cm) of yarn for each st to be cast-on, make a slipknot in the yarn and place it on the right-hand needle, with the tail to the front and the working end to the back. Insert the thumb and forefinger of your left hand between the strands of yarn so that the working end is around your forefinger, and the tail end is around your thumb "slingshot" fashion; *insert the tip of the right–hand needle into the front loop on the thumb, hook the strand of yarn coming from the forefinger from back to front, and draw it through the loop on your thumb; remove your thumb from the loop and pull on the working yarn to tighten the new st on the right–hand needle; return your thumb and forefinger to their original positions, and repeat from * for remaining sts to be CO.

Sloped BO – To eliminate the stair-step look of standard bind-offs along a neck, armhole, or shoulder edge, work the sloped bind-off as follows: Bind off the first row in the usual manner. On the following row, work to the last stitch, slip the last stitch purlwise, turn. Slip the first two stitches purlwise, then pass the first slipped stitch over the last stitch to bind off the first stitch. Continue binding off the rest of the stitches in the usual manner.

YARN RESOURCES

A Verb for Keeping Warm
www.averbforkeepingwarm.com

AngoraGarnet
www.angoragarnet.com

Bare Naked Wools
www.barenakedwools.com

Beaverslide Dry Goods
www.beaverslide.com

Brooklyn Tweed
www.brooklyntweed.com

Buffalo Gold Premium Fibers
stores.buffalogold.net

Cestari Sheep & Wool Company
www.cestarisheep.com

Doc Mason's Wool
www.etsy.com/shop/Odacier

Fancy Tiger Crafts
www.fancytigercrafts.com

Green Mountain Spinnery
www.spinnery.com

Habu Textiles
www.habutextiles.com

Imperial Stock Ranch
www.imperialstockranch.com

Jill Draper Makes Stuff
www.etsy.com/shop/jilldrapermakesstuff

Jones & Vandermeer
www.jonesandvandermeer.com

Julie Asselin
www.julie-asselin.com

Knit Collage
www.knitcollage.com

Malabrigo Yarn
www.malabrigoyarn.com

mYak
www.myak.it

O-Wool
www.o-wool.com

Quince & Co.
www.quinceandco.com

Salt River Mills
www.nasurico.com

Sincere Sheep
www.sinceresheep.com

Starcroft Fiber Mill
www.starcroftfiber.com

The Little Grey Sheep
www.thelittlegreysheep.co.uk

Woolfolk
www.woolfolkyarn.com

INDEX OF DESIGNERS

PAM ALLEN

One of the first knitting books on my bookshelf was Pam Allen's *Knitting for Dummies*. Pam has touched virtually every inch of the yarn industry, from designing and writing, to a term as the editor of *Interweave Knits*, and now produces yarn and patterns for her own brand, Quince & Co. Pam's goal with knitting has always been to encourage more wool production and through this, preserve more green space in the United States. You can follow her most recent endeavors through Quince & Co.'s website: www.quinceandco.com.

VÉRONIK AVERY

French-Canadian designer Véronik Avery is a master of tailoring, construction, and precision. While her designs feel less like handknits and more like professional, couture garments, she writes in an accessible, careful way that allows even adventurous beginners to follow along and achieve beautiful results. She has lent her brilliance to a bevy of knitwear companies, magazines, and books, and has published more than 250 knitwear designs. Each year, knitters can count on Véronik to continually provide garments that are both on trend and classic. Her work and thoughts can be found at: www.veronikavery.com.

JULIA FARWELL-CLAY

Concord, Massachusetts–based designer Julia Farwell-Clay takes on conventional, classic knitwear shapes with new eyes. Her work is simultaneously familiar and fresh, and her patterns are meticulously designed and written to be accessible to a wide range of knitters. Her work has been featured in *Pom Pom Quarterly*, *Knitty*, *Knitscene*, and *PLY*, among others, and her book *From Folly Cove* features a range of imaginative accessories and garments designed in Classic Elite Yarns. Her work can be found on Ravelry and on her website: www.juliafarwellclay.com.

CAROL FELLER

Carol Feller is an independent knitwear designer and teacher residing in Cork, Ireland. Her designs speak to her training in fine art but also to her work as a structural engineer. Her trademarks are seamless construction and clever shaping techniques that result in tailored, interesting garments. Her work has been published in numerous books and magazines, including *Twist Collective*, *Interweave Knits*, *Knitty*, and *Yarn Forward*, and she has several books published in her name. You can follow her work more closely at her blog and website, Stolen Stitches: www.stolenstitches.com.

MEGHAN FERNANDES

The stateside half of the editorial team at *Pom Pom Quarterly*, Meghan Fernandes has brought a wordly and inspiring point of view to her work as a knitwear designer. Her garments and accessories are cozy and modern, vibrant and interesting. Having worked in established London knitting mecca Loop, Meghan has brought delight and whimsy into her work with *Pom Pom Quarterly*, a boutique magazine that is quickly becoming a go-to for fresh knitwear designs: www.pompomquarterly.com.

NORAH GAUGHAN

Few names in the knitting industry are as synonymous with creativity, inspiration, and freshness as Norah Gaughan, a biologist turned knitwear designer. Norah's work stands apart—she has credits in too many places to count, has lent her creative genius to numerous yarn companies, and is the author of *Knitting Nature* and *Norah Gaughan's Knitted Cable Sourcebook,* among others. She lives in New Hampshire and shares her work on her website: www.norahgaughan.net.

BRISTOL IVY

Bristol Ivy's design work focuses on the intersection between innovative technique and classic tailoring. Her creativity and unique approach to knitwear construction have captivated adventurous knitters around the globe. She lives in scenic Portland, Maine, and writes about her travels, career, and random thoughts on her blog: www.bristolivy.com.

KIRSTEN KAPUR

Kirsten Kapur's colorful and exciting take on accessories and garments has been enchanting knitters for over a decade. Kirsten's method of writing is clear, accessible, and encouraging, while communicating complex lace motifs or simple textured stitches. A household name to many knitters, Kirsten's work has been published in over 41 unique publications and through her blog, Through the Loops: www.throughtheloops.com. She lives a colorful life of making in New York, New York, spinning, knitting, drawing, gardening, cooking, and crafting.

MICHELE WANG

Rising star Michele Wang does not design by halves. Her textured garments are heavily adorned with intricate cables, complex lace, and interesting techniques, while her minimalist designs seem effortless and instantly wearable. Michele uses her voice as a designer to support yarns and causes she is passionate about, and has lent her skills to yarn companies with unique fibers and backgrounds. Her work can be found on her website: www.mishi2x.com.

JENNIFER WOOD

Jennifer Wood lives at the foothills of the Blue Ridge Mountains in beautiful Knoxville, Tennessee. A former ballerina and chemist, Jennifer learned to knit for her daughter's school project focused on *The Witch from Blackbird Pond.* Jennifer brings the perfect combination of femininity and elegance to her highly textured, thoughtful designs, and has a vast independently published catalog. She is the author of *Refined Knits,* and her work can be found online at Wood House Knits: www.woodhouseknits.com.

LOCATION: URBAN COWBOY

The Urban Cowboy Bed and Breakfast is a unique space, located in a historic Victorian mansion in East Nashville, Tennessee. It houses eight suites and several communal areas, each decorated meticulously. The style is what the owners like to refer to as "southwestern deco," with hand-applied, hand-printed wallpaper and sculptural wall mosaics created out of reclaimed wood and copper. Owners Jersey Banks and Lyon Porter have created a unique experience for visitors to the city of Nashville with this beautiful space. More information can be found on their website: www.urbancowboybnb.com.

ACKNOWLEDGMENTS

I cannot begin to write down or express my immense gratitude for everyone who was involved in this book's being. I want to first thank my editor, Cristina Garces, who believed in me and this project, and held my hand in many ways through this experience, even when I was occasionally anxiety-ridden and in a panic about minutiae. I have to thank Danielle Young, the graphic designer who remained patient with my nebulous visual revisions, and the amazing team at Abrams that believed in my dream for this book and took a chance on an unknown author. I also have to give so many thanks to my wonderful tech editors, Sue McCain and Therese Chynoweth, who worked to make this vision a complete whole. Without you, this book would not exist at all, and I would never have accomplished it!

Many thanks to the visual team: Katie Meek, my photographer, whose calming presence and assurances made me feel like I could "really do this thing." Joe Gomez, who filmed the promotional pieces for the book, and my models, Sarah and Trish, who were patient, helpful, and went above and beyond to be not only coworkers but friends. I need to give special thanks to our location, the Urban Cowboy Bed and Breakfast—the team there believed in my vision and I was so lucky to be able to shoot in their beautiful space! Additional thanks go to the amazing team at The Blowout Co. in Belle Meade for making everyone look amazing and worthy of the garments, photographer, and space!

I want to thank the industry people who made this possible—all of the designers, dyers, yarn producers, and writers whose work has inspired me and buoyed me toward this project. They are numerous and cannot possibly be listed here. Special thanks are due to Julia, Véronik, Anne, Kirsten, Jennifer, Jinka, Julie, J-F, Annie, Terisa, Ashley, Shaina, Amy, and Mary Catherine. I could not have done without your encouragement and friendship.

To my family, thank you for never questioning, but encouraging, my belief that I could do this project, that someone would be interested in it, and for talking me down every time I called worried that it would never be read. Special thanks to Andrew, who allowed me to put our lives on hold until the final words were written. Thank you to my mother, whose renewed love of knitting has invigorated my own, and my father, who instilled in me a deep love of books and reading. Thank you to my sister, Abigail, whose calm nonchalance at this entire process has made being an author seem like an achievable and reasonable goal. All your pride in what I do is immense and powerful and undeserved. Thank you to Mary Hal Davis,

who taught me how to knit and began this journey. Thank you to the team at Malabrigo Yarn, without whom I never would have begun a career in this industry at all.

Lastly, I thank you, wonderful reader, for picking up this book and reading it to the very end. I hope that it inspires you in the same way that writing it has inspired me. Keep knitting!

ABOUT THE AUTHOR

Hannah Thiessen has been knitting for most of her life and also dabbles in weaving, spinning, painting, quilting, and sewing. When she's not writing, she does freelance marketing, creative direction, social media, and strategy work for yarn companies such as Malabrigo Yarn, Shibui Knits, Zen Yarn Garden, Bare Naked Wools/Knitspot, and Salt River Mills. She blogs online at www.handmadebyhannahbelle.com.